CUTE CROCHETED FOOD

CUTE CROCHETED FOOD

24 TASTY CROCHET DESIGNS!

EMMA VARNAM

THE GUILD OF MASTER CRAFTSMAN PUBLICATIONS

CONTENTS

FRUIT

WATERMELON 24

ORANGE 18

BANANA 34

LEMON 10

CHERRIES 22

PINEAPPLE 14

STRAWBERRY 28

APPLE 30

Check me out

VEGETABLES

AVOCADO 38

BEETROOT 44

PUMPKIN 48

PEAS IN A POD 42

CARROT 50

SWEET TREATS

CROISSANT 56

ICE LOLLIES 66

LEMON AND RAINBOW CAKES 68

ICE-CREAM CONES 58

STRAWBERRY CUPCAKE 78

DOUGHNUTS 74

FAST FOOD

FRIED EGG 102

BURGER AND FRIES 96

PIZZA AND PIZZA SLICES 90

HOT DOG 104

SUSHI 84

INTRODUCTION

I am always so grateful that I discovered the wonderful hobby of crochet. There are so many things you can make with a hook and a strand of yarn. When I want to be cosy, I love making blankets. At other times I am inspired to make hats and scarves for friends. When new babies are on the way there is nothing nicer than making a cute toy for them to cuddle. Every once in a while, a little thought enters my head and I think, 'wouldn't it be fun to make a crocheted cupcake for a party?' and that is how moments of creative whimsy begin. It quite literally is my one and only superpower.

In the last few decades, crochet and toymaking in general has been significantly influenced by Japanese culture. The Japanese technique of 'amigurumi', which is the practice of crocheting in the round, has enabled crocheters to sculpt shapes rather than make items with a number of seams. This technique ensures that toys or decorations are very robust and can be very lifelike.

The Japanese also have a wonderful style of 'kawaii', creating lovable and cute characters out of everyday objects or animals. This works wonderfully for making playful food items: fruit, vegetables and baked goods. Who doesn't want a cute crocheted carrot? When I was a child, I loved playing with food. I had an imaginary kitchen, shop and even a restaurant. All of these patterns would make a fabulous addition to a toy box.

I have had such fun making these patterns. You should feel very sorry for my poor family and friends, who get sent endless photos with the caption, 'isn't this hilarious?'

The most important thing is to stretch your imagination and have fun. Change the colours, alter the expressions and put together a full basket of groceries from your crochet project bag.

FRUIT

LEMON

ZINGY AND ZESTY, THIS LEMON LIVENS UP ANY MEAL. MADE AS EITHER A WHOLE OR A HALF, IT'LL BE A USEFUL ADDITION TO YOUR CROCHETED PRODUCE.

YOU WILL NEED

- Scheepjes Catona, 100% mercerized cotton (68yd/62m per 25g ball):
  1 x 25g ball in 280 Lemon (A)
  A small amount of 205 Kiwi (B), 100 Lemon Chiffon (C) and 106 Snow White (D)
- 3.5mm (UK9:USE/4) crochet hook
- Polyester stuffing
- Tapestry needle
- Pair of ⅛in (4mm) safety eyes
- Strand of black yarn
- Small amount of cardboard

Tension
Tension is not essential for this project.

Finished Size
The lemon is approximately 4¾in (12cm) long.

NOTE The lemon is worked in rounds, using the standard amigurumi technique. Place a marker at the beginning of each round so you know where you are in the pattern.

WHOLE LEMON

Using 3.5mm hook and B, make a magic ring
(see page 117).

Change to A.

Round 1: Ch 1, 6 dc in centre of ring (6 sts).

Round 2: (1 dc, dc2inc) 3 times (9 sts).

Round 3: Work 1 round straight.

Round 4: (2 dc, dc2inc) 3 times (12 sts).

Round 5: (Dc2inc, 1 dc) 6 times (18 sts).

Round 6: (2 dc, dc2inc) 6 times (24 sts).

Round 7: 1 dc, dc2inc, (3 dc, dc2inc) 5 times,
2 dc (30 sts).

Round 8: (Dc2inc, 4 dc) 6 times (36 sts).

Round 9: Work 1 round straight.

Round 10: (5 dc, dc2inc) 6 times ** (42 sts).

Rounds 11–17: Work 7 rounds straight.

Round 18: (5 dc, dc2tog) 6 times (36 sts).

Round 19: Work 1 round straight.

Round 20: (Dc2tog, 4 dc) 6 times (30 sts).

Round 21: Work 1 round straight.

Round 22: 1 dc, dc2tog, (3 dc, dc2tog) 5 times,
2 dc (24 sts).

Stop at this point. Put a safety pin on your
working loop. Using the photograph as a guide,
position and secure safety eyes on the lemon.
Stuff the fruit firmly. Then return to finish
decreasing, putting the working loop back
on your crochet hook.

Round 23: (2 dc, dc2tog) 6 times (18 sts).
Stuff firmly with polyester stuffing.

Round 24: (1 dc, dc2tog) 6 times (12 sts).

Round 25: Work 1 row straight.

Round 26: (Dc2tog) 6 times (6 sts).

Using a tapestry needle, weave this yarn
through the last dc sts of the round and
gather together to close the hole. Fasten
off and weave in ends. Using the photograph
as a guide, stitch the mouth using black yarn.
Using a small amount of B, stitch 5 small
stitches in the end of round 26.

HALF LEMON

Work the whole lemon pattern up until **.
Rounds 11–15: Work 5 rounds straight.
Round 16: 1 dc blo in each st.
Fasten off.

OPEN HALF

Using 3.5mm hook and C, make a magic ring (see page 117).
Round 1: Ch 1, 8 dc in centre of ring (8 sts).
Round 2: 2 dc in each st (16 sts).
Round 3: (Dc2inc, 1 dc) 8 times (24 sts).
Round 4: (2 dc, dc2inc) 8 times (32 sts).
Round 5: 1 dc, dc2inc, (3 dc, dc2inc) 7 times, 2 dc (40 sts).
Round 6: (19 dc, dc2inc) twice (42 sts).
Change to D.
Round 7: Work 1 row straight. Fasten off. Using the photograph as a guide, surface slip stitch 3 lines across the crochet (see page 121). Weave in ends.

MAKING UP

Stuff the body of the lemon firmly. Cut a small circle of cardboard, about 2¾in (7cm) in diameter. Place the cardboard on top of the stuffing. Then place the open half of the lemon on top. Using A, sl st the last row of the lemon half and the last row of the open half together through the back loop. Fasten off and weave in the ends.

ZESTY

PINEAPPLE

THIS FUNKY LITTLE FRUIT IS LOVED THE WORLD OVER FOR ITS ICONIC SHAPE AND TROPICAL TASTE. PERFECT FOR ANYONE WHO WANTS A CHALLENGE, THE SEGMENTS ARE MADE USING A FAN CLUSTER.

YOU WILL NEED

- Scheepjes Secret Garden, 60% polyester, 20% silk, 20% cotton (102yd/93m per 50g ball):
  1 x 50g ball in 707 Summer House (A)
- Scheepjes Metropolis, 75% wool, 25% nylon (219yd/200m per 50g ball):
  1 x 50g ball in 032 Abu Dhabi (B)
  1 x 50g ball in 026 Depok (C)
- 3mm (UK10:USD/3) crochet hook
- 3.5mm (UK9:USE/4) crochet hook
- Polyester stuffing
- Tapestry needle
- Pair of ³/₈in (10mm) safety eyes
- Strand of black yarn

Tension
Tension is not essential for this project.

Finished Size
The pineapple is about 4in (10cm) wide and 10in (25cm) tall.

NOTE The pineapple is worked in rounds. It starts by using simple double crochet stitches and then works fan stitches in continuous rounds. For the main pattern of the pineapple, yarn A and B are used on alternate rounds. When a yarn is not being used, do not cut it off but pull it up through the inside of the work. Place a marker at the beginning of each round so you know where you are in the pattern.

PINEAPPLE
Using 3.5mm hook and A, make a magic ring (see page 117).
Round 1: Ch 1, 6 dc in centre of ring (6 sts).
Round 2: 2 dc in each st (12 sts).
Round 3: (Dc2inc, 1 dc) 6 times (18 sts).
Round 4: (2 dc, dc2inc) 6 times (24 sts).
Round 5: 1 dc, dc2inc, (3 dc, dc2inc) 5 times, 2 dc (30 sts).
Round 6: (Dc2inc, 4 dc) 6 times (36 sts).
Now begin to work the fan clusters.
Round 7: (Miss 1 st, 5 tr in next st, miss 1 st, 1 dc in next st) 9 times (9 fan clusters).
Do not fasten off. Keep yarn at back of the work.

Round 8: Join yarn B, 1 sl st in any st, 1 ch, 1 dc at base of ch, 1 dc in each st (54 sts).
Do not fasten off yarn but keep it to the back of your work.
Change to A.
Round 9: Ch 3 (counts as first st), 2 dtr in first dc of previous round, miss 2 dc, 1 dc in dc sitting on top of 3rd tr of fan, *miss 2 dc, 6 dtr in next dc, miss 2 dc, 1 dc in next st; rep from * 7 times, 3 dtr in first st, join with a sl st to the top of 3 ch, do not fasten off (9 fan clusters).
Change to B.
Round 10: Ch 1, 1 dc at base of ch, 1 dc in each st (63 sts).
Change to A.
Round 11: 1 dc between 3rd and 4th dc of fan of previous round, *miss 3 dc, 6 dtr in next st, miss 3 dc, 1 dc in next st; rep from * 8 times, do not fasten off (9 fan clusters).
Change to B.
Round 12: Ch 1, 1 dc at base of ch, 1 dc in each st. (63 sts).
Rounds 9-12 form the pattern, rep 3 times.
Round 25: Ch 3 (counts as first st), 1 dtr, miss 3 dc, 1 dc in next st, *miss 3 dc, 5 dtr in between sts, miss 3 dc, 1 dc in next st; rep from * 7 times, 3 dtr in first st, join with a sl st to the top of 3 ch, do not fasten off. (9 fan clusters)
Change to B.
Round 26: Ch 1, 1 dc at base of ch, 1 dc in each st. (54 sts). Fasten off yarn B.
Change to A.
Round 27: 1 dc between 2nd and 3rd dc of fan of previous round, miss 3 dc, *4 dtr, miss 2 dc, 1 dc in next st, rep from * 8 times, do not fasten off (9 fan clusters).
Round 28: Ch 1, 1 dc in each st (45 sts).
Round 29: (3 dc, dc2tog) 9 times (36 sts).
Round 30: (2 dc, dc2tog) 9 times (27 sts).
Round 31: (1 dc, dc2tog) 9 times (18 sts).
Fasten off. Using the photograph as a guide, position and secure safety eyes on the pineapple. Stitch the mouth using black yarn. Stuff the fruit firmly.

LARGE LEAF (MAKE 3)

Using 3mm hook and C, make a magic ring (see page 117).

Round 1: Ch 1, 6 dc in centre of ring (6 sts).
Round 2: (2 dc, dc2inc) twice (8 sts).
Round 3: (3 dc, dc2inc) twice (10 sts).
Round 4: (4 dc, dc2inc) twice (12 sts).
Round 5: (5 dc, dc2inc) twice (14 sts).
Round 6: (6 dc, dc2inc) twice (16 sts).
Rounds 7–28: Work 22 rounds straight.
Fasten off, leaving an 8in (20cm) tail of yarn.
Flatten leaf.

MEDIUM LEAF (MAKE 3)

Using 3mm hook and C, make a magic ring (see page 117).

Round 1: Ch 1, 6 dc in centre of ring (6 sts).
Round 2: (2 dc, dc2inc) twice (8 sts).
Round 3: (3 dc, dc2inc) twice (10 sts).
Round 4: (4 dc, dc2inc) twice (12 sts).
Round 5: (5 dc, dc2inc) twice (14 sts).
Round 6: (6 dc, dc2inc) twice (16 sts).
Rounds 7–21: Work 15 rounds straight.
Fasten off, leaving an 8in (20cm) tail of yarn.
Flatten leaf.

LEAF (MAKE 3)

Using 3mm hook and C, make a magic ring (see page 117).

Round 1: Ch 1, 6 dc in centre of ring (6 sts).
Round 2: (2 dc, dc2inc) twice (8 sts).
Round 3: (3 dc, dc2inc) twice (10 sts).
Round 4: (4 dc, dc2inc) twice (12 sts).
Round 5: (5 dc, dc2inc) twice (14 sts).
Round 4: (4 dc, dc2inc) twice (12 sts).
Round 6: (6 dc, dc2inc) twice (16 sts).
Rounds 7–14: Work 8 rounds straight.
Fasten off, leaving an 8in (20cm) tail of yarn.
Flatten leaf.

MAKING UP

Arrange three large leaves together, then surround these with three medium leaves, and then the three small leaves. Sew the leaves together at the base with small stitches. Push the base of the leaves into the hole at the top of the pineapple. Sew the top of the pineapple to the base of the leaves using a strand of yarn A. Sew a leaf firmly at the base of the stem.

TROPICAL

ORANGE

AN ORANGE IS ALWAYS NEEDED FOR SQUEEZING INTO A REFRESHING DRINK. THIS CHEEKY CHAP HAS JUST BEEN PICKED FROM THE TREE AND STILL HAS HIS LEAVES ATTACHED.

YOU WILL NEED

- Scheepjes Catona, 100% mercerized cotton (137yd/125m per 50g ball):
  1 x 50g ball in 281 Tangerine (A)
  A small amount of 515 Emerald (B)
- Scheepjes Metropolis, 75% wool, 25% nylon (219yd/200m per 50g ball):
  A small amount of 066 Copenhagen (C)
- 3mm (UK10:USD/3) crochet hook
- 3.5mm (UK9:USE/4) crochet hook
- Polyester stuffing
- Tapestry needle
- Pair of $^1/_8$in (4mm) safety eyes
- Small amount of floristry wire
- Strand of black yarn

Tension
Tension is not essential for this project.

Finished Size
The orange is approximately $3^1/_2$in (9cm) in diameter.

NOTE The orange is worked in rounds, using the standard amigurumi technique. Place a marker at the beginning of each round so you know where you are in the pattern.

ORANGE

Using 3.5mm hook and B, make a magic ring (see page 117).

Round 1: Ch 1, 6 dc in centre of ring (6 sts). Change to A.

Round 2: 2 dc blo in each st (12 sts).

Round 3: (Dc2inc, 1 dc) 6 times (18 sts).

Round 4: (2 dc, dc2inc) 6 times (24 sts).

Round 5: 1 dc, dc2inc, (3 dc, dc2inc) 5 times, 2 dc (30 sts).

Round 6: (Dc2inc, 4 dc) 6 times (36 sts).

Round 7: (5 dc, dc2inc) 6 times (42 sts).

Round 8: 3 dc, dc2inc (6 dc, dc2inc) 5 times, 3 dc (48 sts).

Rounds 9–17: Work 9 rounds straight.

Round 18: 3 dc, dc2tog (6 dc, dc2tog) 5 times, 3 dc (42 sts).

Round 19: (5 dc, dc2tog) 6 times (36 sts).

Round 20: (Dc2tog, 4 dc) 6 times (30 sts).

Round 21: 1 dc, dc2tog, (3 dc, dc2tog) 5 times, 2 dc (24 sts).

Stop at this point. Put a safety pin on your working loop. Using the photograph as a guide, position and secure safety eyes on to the orange. Stuff the fruit firmly. Then return to finish decreasing, putting the working loop back on your crochet hook.

Round 22: (2 dc, dc2tog) 6 times (18 sts).

Round 23: (1 dc, dc2tog) 6 times (12 sts).

Round 24: (Dc2tog) 6 times (6 sts).

Using a tapestry needle, weave this yarn through the last dc sts of the round and gather together to close the hole. Fasten off and weave in ends. Using the photograph as a guide, stitch the mouth using black yarn.

Squeeze me!

LEAF (MAKE 2)

Using 3mm hook and B, make 7 ch, work around this central ch to make an oval base to the leaf. Work in a continuous spiral placing a maker in the last st of the round.

Round 1: 1 dc in 2nd ch from hook, 1 dc in each of next 5 ch, 1 ch, 1 dc in other side of each 6 ch, 1 ch (14 sts).

Round 2: 6 dc, (1 dc, 1 ch, 1dc) in ch st, 6 dc, join with sl st to ch (17 sts). Fasten off and weave in ends.

STEM

Take a strand of wire and work chain stitches around the wire. Using C and a 3mm hook, place a sl st on your hook. With the wire in the hand that holds your yarn, place the yarn under the wire and your hook over the wire, and yarn over the hook and pull through your sl st. Put your hook under the wire and yarn over, pull up and then put your hook over the wire, yarn over, pull through both loops on the hook. Rep until you have covered the wire as long as you would want it for your stem.

CITRUS

MAKING UP
Push the covered stem through the top of the orange. Sew the base of the step firmly to the top of the orange. Sew two leaves firmly at the base of the stem.

FRESH

CHERRIES

THESE CHERRY TWINS ARE DOUBLE TROUBLE IN THE FRUIT BOWL. THIS PATTERN WOULD BE GREAT MADE UP AS A BROOCH OR BAG CHARM.

CHEEKY

YOU WILL NEED

- Scheepjes Catona, 100% mercerized cotton (68yd/62m per 25g ball):
  1 x 25g ball in 251 Garden Rose (A)
  1 x 25g ball in 515 Emerald (B)
- 3mm (UK10:USD/3) crochet hook
- 3.5mm (UK9:USE/4) crochet hook
- Polyester stuffing
- Tapestry needle
- Pair of 1/8in (4mm) safety eyes
- Small amount of floristry wire
- Strand of black yarn

Tension
Tension is not essential for this project.

Finished Size
Each cherry is approximately 1 1/2in (3.5cm) in diameter.

NOTE The cherries are worked in rounds, using the standard amigurumi technique. Place a marker at the beginning of each round. The stem has a piece of wire in the centre and the crochet is worked around the wire.

CHERRIES
Using 3.5mm hook and A, make a magic ring (see page 117).

Round 1: Ch 1, 6 dc in centre of ring (6 sts).
Round 2: 2 dc in each st (12 sts).
Round 3: (1 dc, dc2inc) 6 times (18 sts).
Round 4: (2 dc, dc2inc) 6 times (24 sts).
Rounds 5–8: Work 4 rounds straight.
Round 9: (2 dc, dc2tog) 6 times (18 sts).
Stop at this point. Put a safety pin on your working loop. Using the photograph as a guide, position and secure safety eyes on the cherry. Stuff the fruit firmly. Then return to finish decreasing, putting the working loop back on your crochet hook.
Round 10: (1 dc, dc2tog) 6 times (12 sts).
Round 11: (Dc2tog) 6 times (6 sts).
Using a tapestry needle, weave this yarn through the last dc sts of the round and gather together to close the hole. Fasten off and weave in ends. Using the photograph as a guide, stitch the mouth using black yarn.

LEAF (MAKE 2)

Using 3mm hook and B, make 10 ch; work around this central ch to make an oval base to the leaf. Work in a continuous spiral, placing a maker in the last st of the round.

Round 1: 1 dc in 2nd ch from hook, 1 dc, 1 htr, 1 tr, 1 dtr, 1 tr, 1 htr, 1 dc, 1 sl st, 1 ch, 1 sl st in other side of each 10 ch, 1 dc, 1 htr, 1 tr, 1 dtr, 1 tr, 1 htr, 2 dc, 1 sl st into turning ch. Fasten off and weave in ends.

STEM

Take a 5in (14cm) strand of wire and work chain stitches around the wire. Using B and a 3mm hook, place a sl st on your hook. With the wire in the hand that holds your yarn, place the yarn under the wire and your hook over the wire. Yarn over the hook and pull through your sl st. Put your hook under the wire and yarn over, pull up and then put your hook over the wire, yarn over, pull through both loops on the hook. Rep until you have covered the wire as long as you would want it for your stem. Bend the wire in half.

MAKING UP

Push the covered stem through the top of each cherry. Sew the base of the stem firmly to the top of each cherry. Sew two leaves firmly at the top of the stem.

SWEET

WATERMELON

JUICY AND REVIVING, THIS MOST TROPICAL OF SNACKS WILL
ALWAYS BE FRESH AND VIBRANT IN ITS CROCHET FORM.

YOU WILL NEED

- Scheepjes Catona, 100% mercerized
  cotton (68yd/62m per 25g ball):
  1 x 25g ball in 114 Shocking pink (A)
  1 x 25g ball in 106 Snow White (B)
  1 x 25g ball in 392 Lime Juice (C)
  1 x 25g ball in 515 Emerald (D)
- 3.5mm (UK9:USE/4) crochet hook
- Polyester stuffing
- Tapestry needle
- Pair of $1/8$in (4mm) safety eyes
- Strand of black yarn

Tension
Tension is not essential for
this project.

Finished Size
The watermelon slice
is approximately
6in (15cm) wide.

JUICY

NOTE The inside of the
watermelon is worked in rounds,
using the standard amigurumi
technique. The outside edge is
worked in rows. Place a marker at
the beginning of each round so you
know where you are in the pattern.

INNER FLESH

Using 3.5mm hook and A, make a magic ring (see page 117).

Round 1: Ch 1, 7 dc in centre of ring (7 sts).

Round 2: 2 dc in each st (14 sts).

Round 3: (Dc2inc, 1 dc) 7 times (21 sts).

Round 4: (2 dc, dc2inc) 7 times (28 sts).

Round 5: 1 dc, dc2inc, (3 dc, dc2inc) 6 times, 2 dc (35 sts).

Round 6: (Dc2inc, 4 dc) 7 times (42 sts).

Round 7: (5 dc, dc2inc) 7 times (49 sts).

Round 8: 3 dc, dc2inc, (6 dc, dc2inc) 6 times, 3 dc (56 sts).

Round 9: (Dc2inc, 7 dc) 7 times (63 sts).

Round 10: (8 dc, dc2inc) 7 times (70 sts).

Round 11: 5 dc, dc2inc, (9 dc, dc2inc) 6 times, 4 dc (77 sts).

Round 12: (10 dc, dc2inc) 7 times (84 sts).
Change to B.

Round 13: (Dc2inc, 11 dc) 7 times (91 sts).
Change to yarn C.

Round 14: 6 dc, dc2inc (12 dc, dc2inc) 6 times, 6 dc (98 sts).
Change to D.

Round 15: Work 1 round straight.
Fasten off and weave in ends.

OUTER RIND

Using 3.5mm hook and D, ch 2 sts.

Row 1: 3 dc in 2nd ch from hook, turn (3 sts).

Row 2: Ch 1, dc2inc, 1 dc, dc2inc, turn (5 sts).

Rows 3–4: Work 2 rows straight, turn.

Row 5: Ch 1, dc2inc, 3 dc, dc2inc, turn (7 sts).

Rows 6–7: Work 2 rows straight, turn.

Row 8: 1ch, dc2inc, 5 dc, dc2inc, turn (9 sts).

Rows 9–40: Work 32 rows straight, turn.

Row 41: Ch 1, dc2tog, 5 dc, dc2inc, turn (7 sts).

Rows 42–43: Work 2 rows straight, turn.

Row 44: Ch 1, dc2tog, 3 dc, dc2inc, turn (5 sts).

Rows 45–46: Work 2 rows straight, turn.

Round 47: Ch 1, dc2tog, 1 dc, dc2inc, turn (3 sts).

Fasten off and weave in ends.

MAKING UP

Fold the inside in half and, using the photograph as a guide, position and secure safety eyes on the side of the slice. Stitch the mouth using black yarn. With wrong sides together; dc the last row of the rind and inner flesh together, leave a small 2in (5cm) hole. Turn the crochet right side out. Stuff the watermelon slice firmly then sew up the final 2in (5cm) hole. Fasten off and weave in ends.

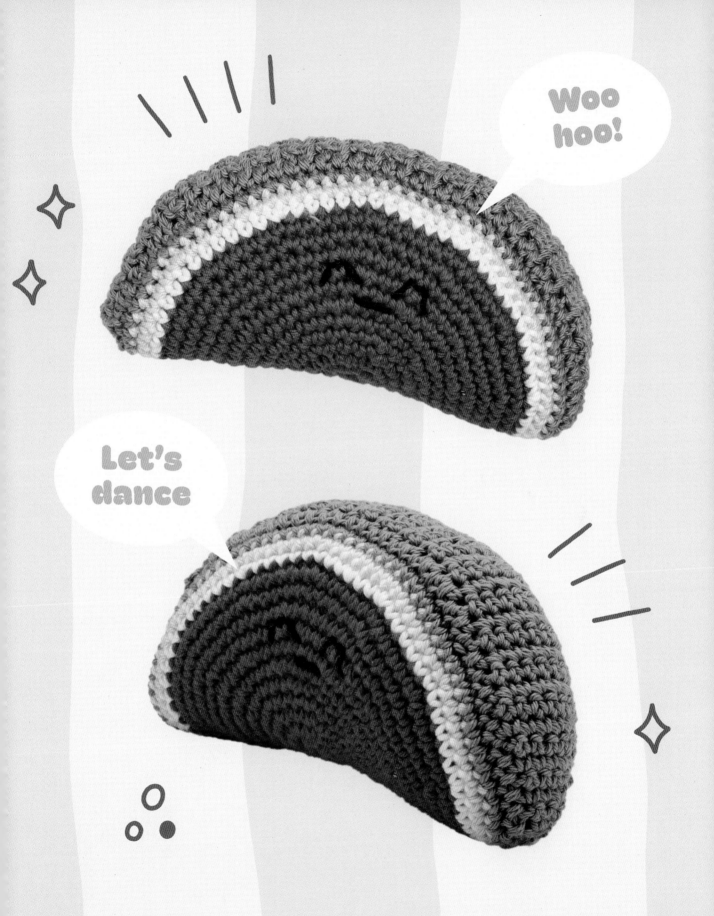

STRAWBERRY

THE FIRST STRAWBERRY OF THE YEAR IS A JOY TO BEHOLD, WHETHER STOLEN FROM THE FRUIT PATCH OR ENJOYED IN A BOWL WITH ICE CREAM. MAKE SEVERAL OF THESE CHEEKY FRUITS AND EMBROIDER A DIFFERENT EXPRESSION ON EACH ONE.

YOU WILL NEED

- Scheepjes Catona, 100% mercerized cotton (137yd/125m per 50g ball):
  1 x 50g ball in 390 Poppy Rose (A)
  1 x 25g ball in 515 Emerald (B)
- 3mm (UK10:USD/3) crochet hook
- 3.5mm (UK9:USE/4) crochet hook
- Polyester stuffing
- Tapestry needle
- Pair of ⅛in 4mm safety eyes
- Strand of black yarn

Tension
Tension is not essential for this project.

Finished Size
The strawberry is approximately 2in (5cm) in diameter.

NOTE The strawberry is worked in rounds, from the bottom up, using the standard amigurumi technique. Place a marker at the beginning of each round. The leaves are worked in a star shape, sl stitches worked into a line of chain stitches.

STRAWBERRY

Using 3.5mm, hook and A,
make a magic ring (see page 117).
Round 1: Ch 1, 5 dc in centre of ring (5 sts).
Round 2: 2 dc in each st (10 sts).
Round 3: (1 dc, dc2inc) 5 times (15 sts).
Round 4: Work 1 row straight.
Round 5: (2 dc, dc2inc) 5 times (20 sts).
Round 6: Work 1 row straight.
Round 7: (3 dc, dc2inc) 5 times (25 sts).
Round 8: Work 1 row straight.
Round 9: (4 dc, dc2inc) 5 times (30 sts).
Rounds 10–11: Work 2 rows straight.
Round 12: (4 dc, dc2tog) 5 times (25 sts).
Round 13: (3 dc, dc2tog) 5 times (20 sts).
Stop at this point. Put a safety pin on your working loop. Using the photograph as a guide, position and secure safety eyes on the strawberry, if you are using them. Stuff the fruit firmly. Then return to finishing the decreasing, putting the working loop back on your crochet hook.
Round 14: (2 dc, dc2tog) 5 times (15 sts).
Round 15: (1 dc, dc2tog) 5 times (10 sts).
Round 16: (Dc2tog) 5 times (5 sts).
Using a tapestry needle, weave this yarn through the last dc sts of the round and gather hole together.
Fasten off and weave in ends.
Using the photograph as a guide, stitch the mouth using black yarn.

STALK

Using 3mm hook and B, make a magic ring
(see page 117).

Round 1: Ch 1, 6 dc in centre of ring (6 sts).

Round 2: 2 dc in each st (12 sts).

Round 3: Ch 6, sl st in 2nd ch from hook,
1 sl st in each of next 4 ch, 1 sl st in st of previous
round, (1 sl st in next st, 6 ch, sl st in 2nd ch from
hook, 1 sl st in each of next 4ch, 1 sl st in next
st of previous round) rep 4 times.

Fasten off and weave in the ends. Sew the stalk
firmly to the top of the strawberry.

APPLE

AN APPLE A DAY KEEPS THE DOCTOR AWAY...
THIS CHEERY GREEN APPLE WOULD ALSO LOOK
WONDERFUL IN ANY PACKED LUNCH AND MIGHT
MAKE A SPECIAL GIFT FOR A TEACHER.

YOU WILL NEED

- *Scheepjes Catona, 100% mercerized cotton (137yd/125m per 50g ball): 1 x 50g ball in 205 Kiwi (A) A small amount of 515 Emerald (B)*
- *3mm (UK10:USD/3) crochet hook*
- *3.5mm (UK9:USE/4) crochet hook*
- *Polyester stuffing*
- *Tapestry needle*
- *Pair of ⅛in (4mm) safety eyes*
- *Small twig*
- *Strand of black yarn*

Tension
Tension is not essential for this project.

Finished Size
- *The apple is approximately 3½in (9cm) in diameter.*

NOTE The apple is worked in rounds, using the standard amigurumi technique. Place a marker at the beginning of each round so you know where you are in the pattern.

APPLE

Using 3.5mm hook and A, make a magic ring (see page 117).

Round 1: Ch 1, 8 dc in centre of ring (8 sts).

Round 2: (3 dc, dc2inc) twice (10 sts).

Round 3: (Dc2inc, 1 dc) 5 times (15 sts).

Round 4: (2 dc, dc2inc) 5 times (20 sts).

Round 5: 1 dc, dc2inc, (3 dc, dc2inc) 4 times, 2 dc (25 sts).

Round 6: (Dc2inc, 4 dc) 5 times (30 sts).

Rounds 7–8: Work 2 rounds straight.

Round 9: (4 dc, dc2inc) 6 times (36 sts).

Round 10: Work 1 round straight.

Round 11: (Dc2inc, 5 dc) 6 times (42 sts).

Rounds 12–13: Work 2 rounds straight.

Round 14: 3 dc, dc2inc (6 dc, dc2inc) 5 times, 3 dc (48 sts).

Rounds 15–17: Work 3 rounds straight.

Round 18: 3 dc, dc2tog (6 dc, dc2tog) 5 times, 3 dc (42 sts).

Round 19: (5 dc, dc2tog) 6 times (36 sts).

Round 20: (Dc2tog, 4 dc) 6 times (30 sts).

Round 21: 1 dc, dc2tog, (3 dc, dc2tog) 5 times, 2 dc (24 sts).

Stop at this point. Put a safety pin on your working loop. Using the photographs as a guide, position and secure safety eyes on the apple. Stuff the fruit firmly. Then return to finish decreasing, putting the working loop back on your crochet hook.

Round 22: (2 dc, dc2tog) 6 times (18 sts).

Round 23: (1 dc, dc2tog) 6 times (12 sts).

Round 24: (Dc2tog) 6 times (6 sts).

Using a tapestry needle, weave this yarn through the last dc sts of the round and gather together to close the hole. Fasten off and weave in ends. Using the photograph as a guide, stitch the mouth using black yarn.

LEAF

Using 3mm hook and B, make 7 ch; work around this central ch to make an oval base to the leaf. Work in a continuous spiral, placing a maker in the last st of the round.

Round 1: 1 dc in 2nd ch from hook, 1 dc in each of next 5 ch, 1 ch, 1 dc in other side of each 6 ch, 1 ch (14 sts).

Round 2: 6 dc, (1 dc, 1 ch, 1 dc) in ch st, 6 dc, join with sl st to ch (16 sts).

Fasten off and weave in ends.

MAKING UP

Push a small twig through the top of the apple. Sew a leaf firmly at the base of the stem.

CRUNCHY

DELICIOUS

BANANA

THE PERFECT SNACK, AND AN INSTANT ENERGY BOOST, THIS CROCHET BANANA IS SURE TO BE LOVED BY ALL.

Top banana

YOU WILL NEED

- *Scheepjes Catona, 100% mercerized cotton (68yd/62m per 25g ball): 1 x 25g ball in 208 Yellow Gold (A) A small amount of 507 Chocolate (B)*
- *3.5mm (UK9:USE/4) crochet hook*
- *Polyester stuffing*
- *Tapestry needle*
- *Pair of ⅛in (4mm) safety eyes*
- *Strand of black yarn*

Tension
Tension is not essential for this project.

Finished Size
- *The banana is approximately 7½in (19cm) long.*

NOTE The banana is worked in rounds using the standard amigurumi technique. The slight bend in the banana is created by using larger stitches on one side. Place a marker at the beginning of each round.

BANANA

Using 3.5mm hook and B, make a magic ring (see page 117).
Round 1: Ch 1, 6 dc in centre of ring (6 sts). Change to A.
Round 2: (1dc, dc2inc) 3 times (9 sts).
Round 3: (2 dc, dc2inc) 3 times (12 sts).
Round 4: (3 dc, dc2inc) 3 times (15 sts).
Rounds 5–6: Work 2 rounds straight in dc.
Round 7: (4 dc, dc2inc) 3 times (18 sts).
Rounds 8–10: Work 3 rounds straight in dc.
Round 11: (5 dc, dc2inc) 3 times (21 sts).
Rounds 12–14: 8 dc, 5 htr, 8 dc.
Rounds 15–17: Work 3 rounds straight in dc.
Rounds 18–21: 9 dc, 5 htr, 7 dc.
Rounds 22–23: Work 2 rounds straight in dc.
Round 24: (5 dc, dc2tog) 3 times (18 sts).
Round 25: 8 dc, 4 htr, 6 dc.
Round 26: Work 1 round straight in dc.
Round 27: (4 dc, dc2tog) 3 times (15 sts).
Round 28: 7 dc, 3 htr, 5 dc.
Round 29: Work 1 round straight in dc.
Round 30: (3 dc, dc2tog) 3 times (12 sts).
Stop at this point. Put a safety pin on your working loop. Using the photograph as a guide, position and secure safety eyes on the banana. Stuff the fruit firmly. Then return to finish decreasing, putting the working loop back on your crochet hook.
Round 31: (Dc2tog) 6 times (6 sts).
Change to B.
Rounds 32–35: Work 4 rounds straight in dc. If you can fit a little more stuffing in the top of the banana, do so. Using a tapestry needle, weave this yarn through the last dc sts of the round and gather together to close the hole. Fasten off and weave in the ends.

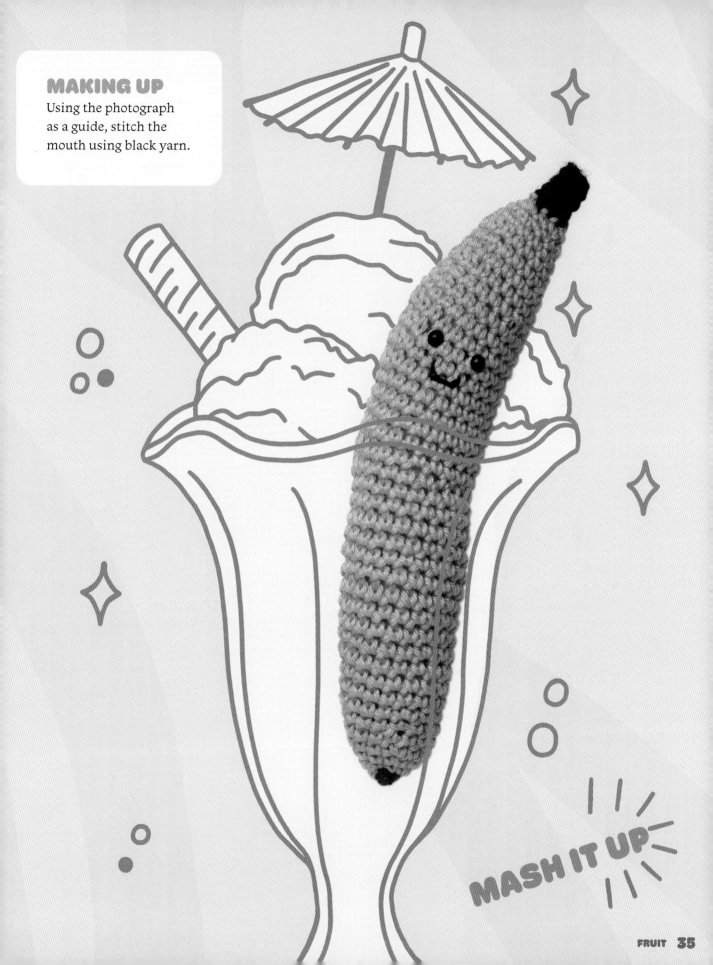

MASH IT UP

AVOCADO

THIS SCRUMMY AVOCADO IS PERFECT FOR A HEALTHY BREAKFAST OR A LIVELY LUNCH. POP THE TUMMY STONE IN AND OUT FOR EXTRA FUN AND GAMES.

YOU WILL NEED

- Scheepjes Catona, 100% mercerized cotton (68yd/62m per 25g ball):
  1 x 25g ball in 392 Lime Juice (A)
  1 x 25g ball in 515 Emerald (B)
  1 x 25g ball in 507 Chocolate (C)
- 3.5mm (UK9:USE/4) crochet hook
- Polyester stuffing
- Tapestry needle
- Pair of ⅛in (4mm) safety eyes
- Strand of black yarn

Tension
Tension is not essential for this project.

Finished Size
The avocado is about 3½in (9cm) wide and 4in (10cm) long.

NOTE The avocado is worked in rounds, using the standard amigurumi technique. The front and the back are worked separately and then joined together in the last row. Place a marker at the beginning of each round.

FRONT

Using 3.5mm hook and A, make a magic ring (see page 117).

Round 1: Ch 1, 6 dc in centre of ring (6 sts).
Round 2: 2 dc in each st (12 sts).
Round 3: (Dc2inc, 1 dc) 6 times (18 sts).
Round 4: (2 dc, dc2inc) 6 times (24 sts).
Rounds 5–7: Work 3 rounds straight.
Round 8: (3 dc, dc2inc blo) 6 times (30 sts).
Round 9: (Dc2inc, 4 dc) 6 times (36 sts).
Round 10: (5 dc, dc2inc) 6 times (42 sts).
You will now work in rows to create the top of the pear shape.
Row 1: Ch 1, 11 dc, turn (11 sts).
Row 2: Ch 1, miss 1, 8 dc, miss 1, 1 dc, turn (9 sts).
Row 3: Ch 1, miss 1, 6 dc, miss 1, 1 dc, turn (7 sts).
Row 4: Ch 1, miss 1, 4 dc, miss 1, 1 dc, turn (5 sts).
Row 5: Ch 1, miss 1, 2 dc, miss 1, 1 dc, turn (3 sts).
Now start to work in rounds again.
With RS facing, change to B.
You will begin to work down the row ends of the left side of the avocado.
Round 1: 1 dc in each of next 4 row ends, work 31 dc, 1 dc in each of next 4 row ends, in last 3 sts work (dc2inc, 1 dc, dc2inc) (44 sts).
Round 2: Work 1 round straight.
Fasten off and weave in ends. Place safety eyes using the photograph as a guide or stitch the eyes and mouth using black yarn.

BACK

Using 3.5mm hook and B, make a magic ring (see page 117).

Round 1: Ch 1, 6 dc in centre of ring (6 sts).

Round 2: 2 dc in each st (12 sts).

Round 3: (Dc2inc, 1 dc) 6 times (18 sts).

Round 4: (2 dc, dc2inc) 6 times (24 sts).

Round 5: (3 dc, dc2inc) 6 times (30 sts).

Round 6: (Dc2inc, 4 dc) 6 times (36 sts).

Round 7: (5 dc, dc2inc) 6 times (42 sts).

Rounds 8–9: Work 2 rounds straight.

You will now work in rows to create the top of the pear shape

Row 1: Ch 1, 11 dc, turn (11 sts).

Row 2: Ch 1, miss 1, 8 dc, miss 1, 1 dc, turn (9 sts).

Row 3: Ch 1, miss 1, 6 dc, miss 1, 1 dc, turn (7 sts).

Row 4: Ch 1, miss 1, 4 dc, miss 1, 1 dc, turn (5 sts).

Row 5: Ch 1, miss 1, 2 dc, miss 1, 1 dc, turn (3 sts).

Now start to work in rounds again. You will begin to work down the row ends of the left side of the avocado.

Round 1: 1 dc in each of next 4 row ends, work 31 dc, 1 dc in each of next 4 row ends, in last 3 sts work (dc2inc, 1 dc, dc2inc) (44 sts).

Round 2: Work 1 round straight.

Do not fasten off, but place stuffing in the back of the avocado, ensuring an indent remains for the stone. With back facing and aligning the shape of the avocado, dc the two sides together.

Yikes!

STONE

Using 3.5mm hook and C, make a magic ring (see page 117).

Round 1: Ch 1, 6 dc in centre of ring (6 sts).

Round 2: 2 dc in each st (12 sts).

Round 3: (1 dc, dc2inc) 6 times (18 sts).

Round 4: (2 dc, dc2inc) 6 times (24 sts).

Rounds 5–6: Work 2 rounds straight.

Round 7: (2 dc, dc2tog) 6 times (18 sts).

Stop at this point. Put a safety pin on your working loop. Stuff the stone firmly. Then return to finish decreasing, putting the working loop back on your crochet hook.

Round 8: (1 dc, dc2tog) 6 times (12 sts).

Round 9: (Dc2tog) 6 times (6 sts).

Using a tapestry needle, weave this yarn through the last dc sts of the round and gather together to close the hole. Fasten off and weave in ends.

MAKING UP

Place the stone in the avocado indent.

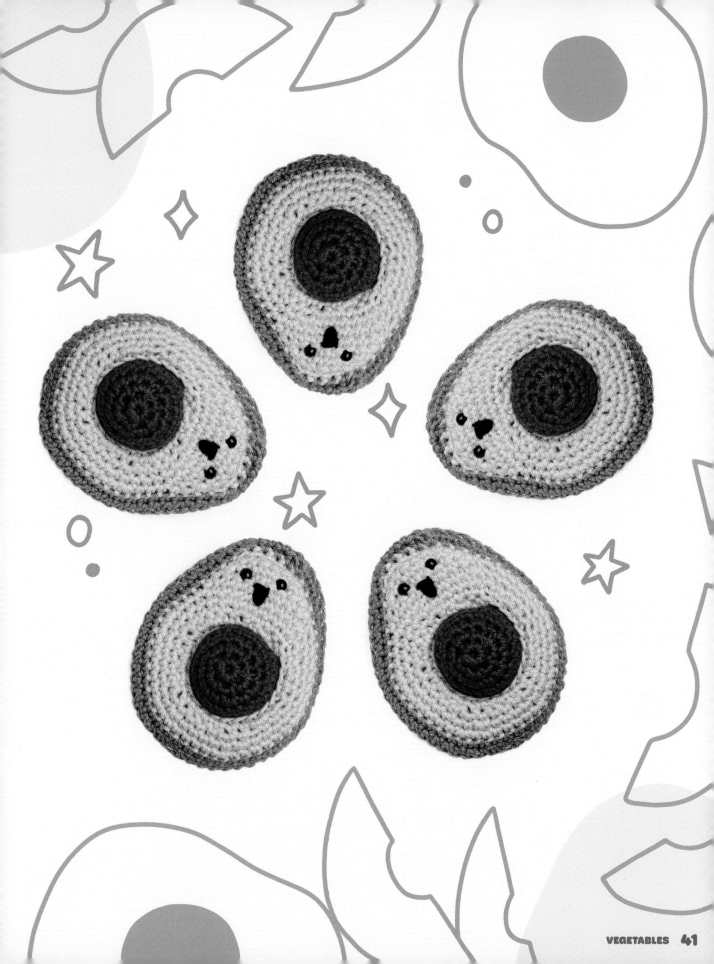

PEAS IN A POD

THESE PEAS LOOK SO COSY IN THEIR LITTLE POD.
CHOOSE HOW YOU WANT TO EMBROIDER THEIR FACES
AS EACH PEA CAN HAVE A UNIQUE EXPRESSION.

YOU WILL NEED

- *Scheepjes Catona, 100% mercerized cotton (68yd/62m per 25g ball):*
  1 x 25g ball in 205 Kiwi (A)
  1 x 25g ball in 515 Emerald (B)
- *3.5mm (UK9:USE/4) crochet hook*
- *Polyester stuffing*
- *Tapestry needle*
- *3 pairs of ¹/₈in (4mm) safety eyes*
- *Small amount of floristry wire*
- *Strand of black yarn*

Tension
*Tension is not essential
for this project.*

Finished Size
*Each pea is approximately
1in (2.5cm) in diameter, the
pod is 4in (10cm) long.*

NOTE The peas are worked
in rounds, using the standard
amigurumi technique. Place a
marker at the beginning of each
round. The pod is worked
as an oval working around
the central chain stitch row.

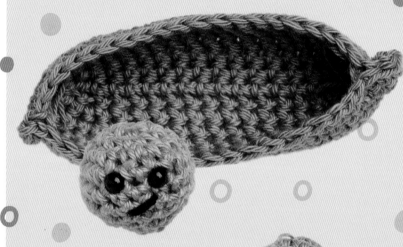

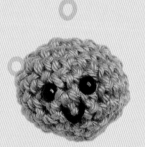

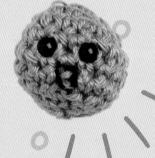

PEA (MAKE 3)

Using 3.5mm hook and A, make a magic ring (see page 117).

Round 1: Ch 1, 6 dc in centre of ring (6 sts).

Round 2: 2 dc in each st (12 sts).

Round 3: (1 dc, dc2inc) 6 times (18 sts).

Rounds 4–6: Work 3 rounds straight.

Stop at this point. Put a safety pin on your working loop. Using the photograph as a guide, position and secure safety eyes on the pea. Stuff firmly. Then return to finish decreasing, putting the working loop back on your crochet hook.

Round 7: (1 dc, dc2tog) 6 times (12 sts).

Round 8: (Dc2tog) 6 times (6 sts).

Using a tapestry needle, weave this yarn through the last dc sts of the round and gather together to close the hole. Fasten off and weave in ends. Using the photograph as a guide, stitch the kind of mouth you choose using black yarn.

POD

Using 3.5mm hook and B, make 15 ch, work around this central ch to make an oval base to the pod. Work in a continuous spiral placing a maker in the last st of the round.

Round 1: 1 dc in 2nd ch from hook, 1 dc in each of next 13 ch, 1 ch, 14 dc in other side of each ch, 1 ch (30 sts).

Round 2: Dc2inc, 12 dc, (dc2inc) 3 times, 12 dc, (dc2inc) twice (36 sts).

Round 3: Dc2inc, 13 dc, (dc2inc, 1 dc) 3 times, 12 dc, (dc2inc, 1 dc) twice (42 sts).

Rounds 4–7: Work 4 rounds straight.

Round 8: (Dc2inc) twice, 18 dc, (dc2inc) 3 times, 18 dc, dc2inc (48 sts).

Fasten off and leave a long tail of yarn. Fold the pod in half and sew 4 sts together at each end of the pod.

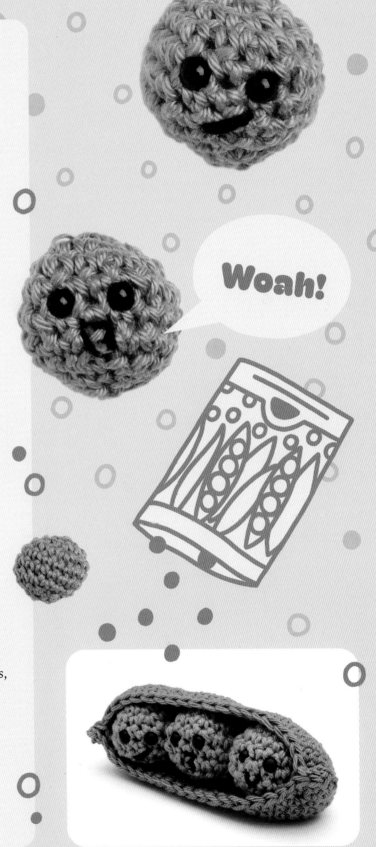

Woah!

BEETROOT

THIS VEGETABLE BRINGS COLOUR AND FLAVOUR TO THE VEGETABLE PATCH. IT'S A LOVELY COMPANION FOR SALADS OR ROASTED FOR WINTER COMFORT FOOD.

YOU WILL NEED

- *Scheepjes Catona, 100% mercerized cotton (68yd/62m per 25g ball):*
  1 x 25g ball in 251 Garden Rose (A)
  1 x 25g ball in 244 Spruce (B)
- *3mm (UK10:USD/3) crochet hook*
- *3.5mm (UK9:USE/4) crochet hook*
- *Polyester stuffing*
- *Tapestry needle*
- *Pair of 1/4in (6mm) safety eyes*
- *Strand of black yarn*

Tension

Tension is not essential for this project.

Finished Size

The beetroot is approximately 2in (5cm) in diameter.

NOTE The beetroot is worked in rounds starting from the top and working down, using the standard amigurumi technique. Place a marker at the beginning of each round. The stem of the leaf is worked in yarn A and the actual leaf is worked in yarn B.

BEETROOT

Using 3.5mm hook and A, make a magic ring (see page 117).

Round 1: Ch 1, 6 dc in centre of ring (6 sts).

Round 2: 2 dc in each st (12 sts).

Round 3: (1 dc, dc2inc) 6 times (18 sts).

Round 4: (2 dc, dc2inc) 6 times (24 sts).

Round 5: (3 dc, dc2inc) 6 times (30 sts).

Rounds 6–11: Work 6 rounds straight.

Round 12: (4 dc, dc2tog) 5 times (25 sts).

Round 13: Work 1 round straight.

Round 14: (3 dc, dc2tog) 5 times (20 sts).

Round 15: Work 1 round straight.

Round 16: (2 dc, dc2tog) 5 times (15 sts).

Stop at this point. Put a safety pin on your working loop. Using the photograph as a guide, position and secure safety eyes on the beetroot. Stuff firmly. Then return to finish decreasing, putting the working loop back on your crochet hook.

Round 17: Work 1 round straight.

Round 18: (1 dc, dc2tog) 5 times (10 sts).

Round 19: (Dc2tog) 5 times (5 sts).

Using a tapestry needle, weave this yarn through the last dc sts of the round and gather together to close the hole. Using A, make 3 loops approx. ⅜in (1cm) long at the base of the beetroot. Fasten off and weave in ends. Cut the middle of all 3 loops to make 6 strands, then use a tapestry needle to pull out the fibres of the strands to create roots. Using the photograph as a guide, stitch the mouth using black yarn.

SLURP

LEAF (MAKE 3)

Using 3mm hook and A, make 19 ch.

Round 1: 1 sl st in 2nd ch from hook, 7 sl st, change to yarn B. 1 dc, 1 htr, tr2inc, dtr2inc, tr2inc, 2 htr, tr2inc, dtr2inc, (5tr in last ch st) now work in other side of ch sts, dtr2inc, tr2inc, 2 htr, tr2inc, dtr2inc, tr2inc, 1 htr, 1 dc. Fasten off and weave in the ends.

MAKING UP

Sew the base of each leaf stem firmly to the top of the beetroot. Fasten off and weave in the ends.

MUNCH

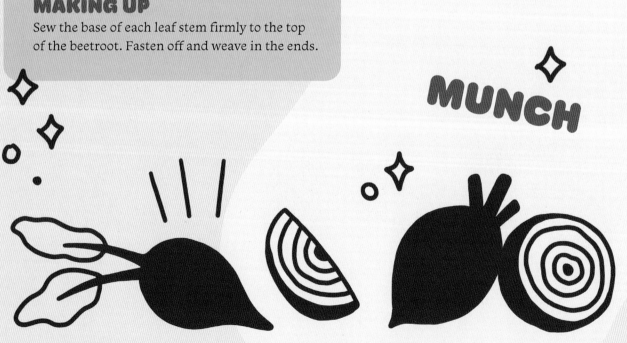

PUMPKIN

NOTHING IS MORE CHEERING ON AN AUTUMN DAY THAN A PUMPKIN. THIS PATTERN IS NOT ONLY CUDDLY BUT ALSO MAKES A WONDERFUL DECORATION FOR HOLIDAY FESTIVITIES.

Spooky!

YOU WILL NEED

- Stylecraft Naturals Organic Cotton, 100% cotton (114yd/105m per 50g ball): 1 x 50g ball in 7181 Carrot (A) 1 x 50g ball in 7189 Coffee Bean (B)
- 3.5mm (UK9:USE/4) crochet hook
- Polyester stuffing
- Pair of ⁵/₁₆in (8mm) plastic safety eyes
- Tapestry needle
- Strand of black yarn

Tension
Tension is not essential for this project.

Finished Size
The pumpkin is approximately 4in (10cm) in diameter.

NOTE The pumpkin is worked in rows. The rib is created by working into the back loop of each stitch (see page 119).

PUMPKIN

Using 3.5mm hook and A, ch 22 sts.
Row 1 (WS): 1 htr in 3rd ch from hook, 2 htr, 14 tr, 3 htr, turn (20 sts).
Row 2: Ch 2 (counts as first st), 2 htr blo, 14 tr blo, 3 htr blo, turn (20 sts).
Row 2 forms the pattern. Work a further 26 rows. With RS together now crochet the first and last rows together:
Next row: Ch 1, sl st in every st.
Fasten off and leave a long tail.

STALK

Using 3.5mm hook and B, make a magic ring (see page 117).

Round 1: Ch 1, 6 dc in centre of ring (6 sts).

Rounds 2–4: Work 3 rounds straight.

Fasten off, leaving a long tail of yarn.

MAKING UP

Sew small running stitches along one side seam and then gather the end together to form the top of the pumpkin. Sew the base of the stalk to the centre of the gathered stitches. Place the safety eyes on the side of the pumpkin. Firmly stuff the pumpkin, then gather together the stitches of the open end to form a ball. Using a tapestry needle and black yarn, sew the mouth using small stitches.

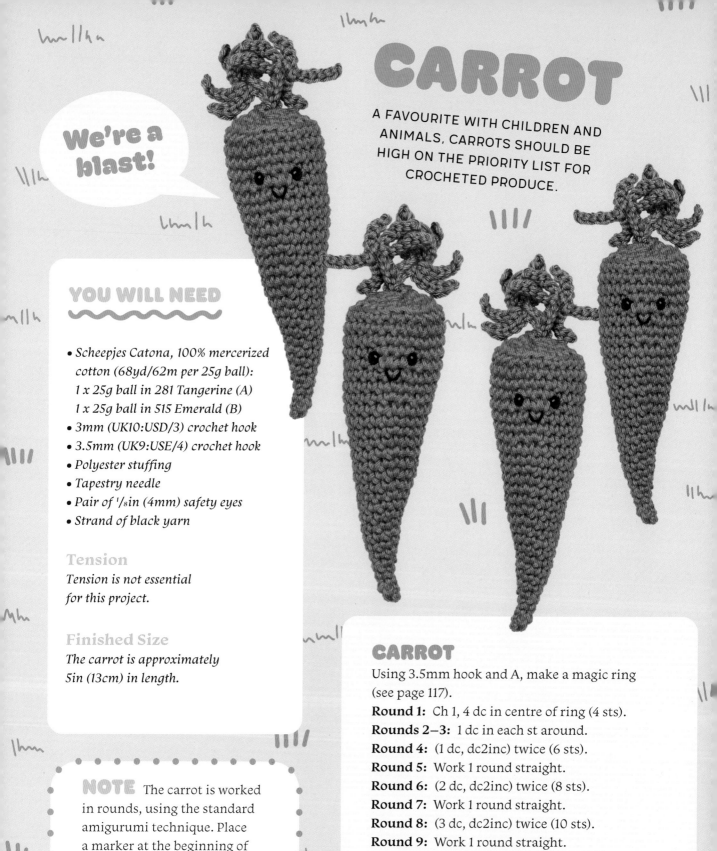

CARROT

A FAVOURITE WITH CHILDREN AND ANIMALS, CARROTS SHOULD BE HIGH ON THE PRIORITY LIST FOR CROCHETED PRODUCE.

We're a blast!

YOU WILL NEED

- Scheepjes Catona, 100% mercerized cotton (68yd/62m per 25g ball):
  1 x 25g ball in 281 Tangerine (A)
  1 x 25g ball in 515 Emerald (B)
- 3mm (UK10:USD/3) crochet hook
- 3.5mm (UK9:USE/4) crochet hook
- Polyester stuffing
- Tapestry needle
- Pair of ⅛in (4mm) safety eyes
- Strand of black yarn

Tension
Tension is not essential for this project.

Finished Size
The carrot is approximately 5in (13cm) in length.

NOTE The carrot is worked in rounds, using the standard amigurumi technique. Place a marker at the beginning of each round.

CARROT

Using 3.5mm hook and A, make a magic ring (see page 117).

Round 1: Ch 1, 4 dc in centre of ring (4 sts).
Rounds 2–3: 1 dc in each st around.
Round 4: (1 dc, dc2inc) twice (6 sts).
Round 5: Work 1 round straight.
Round 6: (2 dc, dc2inc) twice (8 sts).
Round 7: Work 1 round straight.
Round 8: (3 dc, dc2inc) twice (10 sts).
Round 9: Work 1 round straight.
Round 10: (4 dc, dc2inc) twice (12 sts).
Round 11: Work 1 round straight.

Round 12: (5 dc, dc2inc) twice (14 sts).
Round 13: Work 1 round straight.
Round 14: (6 dc, dc2inc) twice (16 sts).
Round 15: Work 1 round straight.
Round 16: (7 dc, dc2inc) twice (18 sts).
Round 17: Work 1 round straight.
Round 18: (8 dc, dc2inc) twice (20 sts).
Round 19: Work 1 round straight.
Round 20: (9 dc, dc2inc) twice (22 sts).
Round 21: Work 1 round straight.
Round 22: (10 dc, dc2inc) twice (24 sts).

Round 23: (2 dc, dc2tog blo) 6 times (18 sts). Stop at this point. Put a safety pin on your working loop. Using the photograph as a guide, position and secure safety eyes on the carrot. Stuff the carrot firmly. Then return to finish decreasing, putting the working loop back on your crochet hook.
Round 24: (1 dc, dc2tog) 6 times (12 sts).
Round 25: (Dc2tog) 6 times (6 sts). Leave a long tail of yarn and do not close the hole in the top of the carrot.

CRUNCHY

LEAF (MAKE 2)

Using 3mm hook and B, make 7 ch.
Row 1: 1 dc in 2nd ch from hook, 1 sl st in each of next 5 ch, (6 ch, sl st in 2nd ch from hook, 1 sl st in each of next 4ch) rep 4 more times. Fasten off and weave in ends. The longer strand is the stem.

MAKING UP

Push both stems of each leaf through the top of the carrot. Sew the base of the stem firmly to the top of the carrot. Using the photographs as a guide, stitch the mouth using black yarn.

PARTY

WHOOP

Wake up!

CROISSANT

RISE AND SHINE WITH THIS CRUNCHY
AND BUTTERY BREAKFAST FEAST –
DELICIOUS DUNKED IN A CUP
OF HOT CHOCOLATE.

YOU WILL NEED

- Sirdar Haworth Tweed DK,
  50% nylon, 50% wool
  (180yd/165m per 50g ball):
  1 x 50g ball in 910 Harewood
  Chestnut (A)
- 3.5mm (UK9:USE/4) crochet hook
- Polyester stuffing
- Tapestry needle
- Pair of 6mm safety eyes
- Strand of black yarn

Tension
*Tension is not essential
for this project.*

Finished Size
*The croissant is
approximately 6¹/₂in
(17cm) long.*

NOTE The two points of
the croissant are worked in
rounds, using the standard
amigurumi technique. The
outside of the croissant is
created by making a long
piece of crochet worked in
rows. Place a marker at the
beginning of each round so
you know where you are
in the pattern.

BON APPÉTIT!

CROISSANT POINTS (MAKE 2)

Using 3.5mm hook and A, make a magic ring (see page 117).

Round 1: Ch 1, 8 dc in centre of ring (8 sts).
Round 2: (Dc2inc, 1 dc) 4 times (12 sts).
Round 3: Work 1 round straight.
Round 4: (2 dc, dc2inc) 4 times (16 sts).
Rounds 5–7: Work 3 rounds straight.
Round 8: (3 dc, dc2inc) 4 times (20 sts).
Rounds 9–18: Work 10 rounds straight.
Fasten off and weave in ends.

OUTER PASTRY

Using 3.5mm hook and A, ch 2 sts.

Row 1: 3 dc in 2nd ch from hook, turn (3 sts).
Row 2: Work 1 row straight.
Row 3: Ch 1, dc2inc, 1 dc, dc2inc, turn (5 sts).
Row 4: Work 1 row straight, turn.
Row 5: Ch 1, dc2inc, 3 dc, dc2inc, turn (7 sts).
Row 6: Work 1 row straight, turn.
Row 7: Ch 1, dc2inc, 5 dc, dc2inc, turn (9 sts).
Row 8: Work 1 row straight, turn.
Row 9: Ch 1, dc2inc, 7 dc, dc2inc, turn (11 sts).
Rows 10–24: Work 15 rows straight, turn.
Row 25: Ch 1, dc2inc, 9 dc, dc2inc, turn (13 sts).
Row 26: Work 1 row straight, turn.
Row 27: Ch 1, dc2inc, 7 dc, dc2inc, turn (15 sts).
Row 28: Work 1 row straight, turn.
Row 29: Ch 1, dc2inc, 7 dc, dc2inc, turn (17 sts).
Row 30: Work 1 row straight, turn.
Rows 31–48: Work 18 rows straight, turn.
Fasten off and weave in the ends.

MAKING UP

Stuff both points and then, using a tail of yarn A, whip stitch both last rows of the points together. Taking the last row of the pastry outer, sew this at the back of the croissant. Roll the pastry over the centre join of the croissant points, sewing the row sides to the inner as you go. Near to the beginning of the pastry outer, secure the safety eyes, using the photograph as a guide. Then sew down the last part of the pastry. Stitch the mouth using black yarn.

ICE-CREAM CONES

THERE ARE SO MANY WAYS TO CREATE YOUR FAVOURITE MOUTHWATERING ICE CREAM IN A CONE. DO YOU FAVOUR A WHIPPY WITH A FLAKE, A LOVELY STRAWBERRY ICE CREAM OR EVEN A ZINGY BLUE RASPBERRY FLAVOUR?

YOU WILL NEED

- Sirdar Snuggly 100% cotton DK, 100% cotton (116yd/106m per 50g ball):
  1 x 50g ball in 773 Fawn (A)
- Sirdar Snuggly Bunny, 100% nylon (98yd/90m per 50g ball):
  1 x 50g ball in 314 Piglet (B)
  1 x 50g ball in 310 Lamb (C)
- Sirdar Happy Cotton, 100% cotton (47yd/43m per 20g ball):
  1 x 20g ball in 762 Shower (D)
  1 x 20g ball in 789 Lippy (E)
  1 x 20g ball in 777 Cookie (F)
  Small amount in 780 Treetop (G)
- Sirdar Happy Chenille, 100% polyester (41yd/38m per 15g ball):
  1 x 15g ball in 0013 Fuzzy (H)
  1 x 15g ball in 0026 Splash (I)
- 3.5mm (UK9:USE/4) crochet hook
- Polyester stuffing
- Tapestry needle
- Pair of 1/8in (4mm) safety eyes
- Strand of black yarn

Tension
Tension is not essential for this project.

Finished Size
The strawberry ice cream is approximately 8in (20cm) tall.
The whippy ice cream is approximately 8³⁄₄in (22cm) tall.

NOTE The ice cream and cones are worked in rounds, using the standard amigurumi technique. The fluffy yarn is harder to see where to place you hook, however it is easier to feel with your fingers where each stitch should be placed. Place a marker at the beginning of each round so you know where you are in the pattern.

CONE (MAKE 2)

Using 3.5mm hook and A, make a magic ring
(see page 117).

Round 1: Ch 1, 6 dc in centre of ring (6 sts).
Round 2: Work 1 round straight.
Round 3: (Dc2inc, 1 dc) 3 times (9 sts).
Round 4: Work 1 round straight.
Round 5: (2 dc, dc2inc) 3 times (12 sts).
Round 6: Work 1 round straight.
Round 7: (3 dc, dc2inc) 3 times (15 sts).
Round 8: Work 1 round straight.
Round 9: (Dc2inc, 4 dc) 3 times (18 sts).
Round 10: Work 1 round straight.
Round 11: (5 dc, dc2inc) 3 times (21 sts).
Round 12: Work 1 round straight.
Round 13: (6 dc, dc2inc) 3 times (24 sts).
Round 14: Work 1 round straight.
Round 15: (7 dc, dc2inc) 3 times (27 sts).
Round 16: Work 1 round straight.
Round 17: (8 dc, dc2inc) 3 times (30 sts).
Rounds 18–19: Work 2 rounds straight.
Round 20: Ch 2 (counts as first tr),
1 tr in each st around (30 sts).
Round 21: 1 dc blo in each st around.
Round 22: Work 1 round in crab stitch
(see page 120). Fasten off and leave
a 12in (30cm) tail of yarn.

I'm too cute!

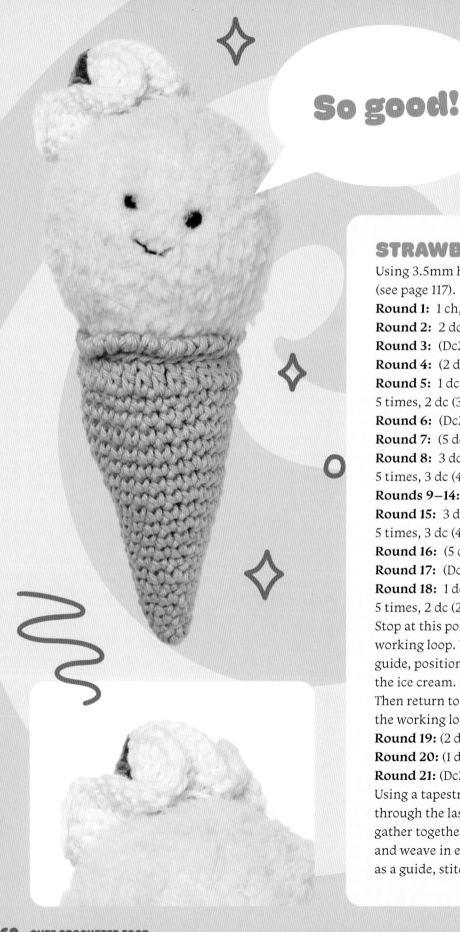

So good!

STRAWBERRY ICE CREAM

Using 3.5mm hook and B, make a magic ring (see page 117).

Round 1: 1 ch, 6 dc in centre of ring (6 sts).

Round 2: 2 dc in each st (12 sts).

Round 3: (Dc2inc, 1 dc) 6 times (18 sts).

Round 4: (2 dc, dc2inc) 6 times (24 sts).

Round 5: 1 dc, dc2inc, (3 dc, dc2inc) 5 times, 2 dc (30 sts).

Round 6: (Dc2inc, 4 dc) 6 times (36 sts).

Round 7: (5 dc, dc2inc) 6 times (42 sts).

Round 8: 3 dc, dc2inc (6 dc, dc2inc) 5 times, 3 dc (48 sts).

Rounds 9–14: Work 6 rounds straight.

Round 15: 3 dc, dc2tog (6 dc, dc2tog) 5 times, 3 dc (42 sts).

Round 16: (5 dc, dc2tog) 6 times (36 sts).

Round 17: (Dc2tog, 4 dc) 6 times (30 sts).

Round 18: 1 dc, dc2tog, (3 dc, dc2tog) 5 times, 2 dc (24 sts).

Stop at this point. Put a safety pin on your working loop. Using the photograph as a guide, position and secure safety eyes on the ice cream. Stuff the ice cream firmly. Then return to finish decreasing, putting the working loop back on your crochet hook.

Round 19: (2 dc, dc2tog) 6 times (18 sts).

Round 20: (1 dc, dc2tog) 6 times (12 sts).

Round 21: (Dc2tog) 6 times (6 sts).

Using a tapestry needle, weave this yarn through the last dc sts of the round and gather together to close the hole. Fasten off and weave in ends. Using the photograph as a guide, stitch the mouth using black yarn.

WHIPPED CREAM

Using 3.5mm hook and D, make a magic ring
(see page 117).

Round 1: Ch 1, 6 dc in centre of ring (6 sts).

Round 2: 2 dc in each st (12 sts).

Round 3: Ch 3 (counts as first st) 2 tr in st
at base of ch, 3 tr in each st around,
join with a sl st to 3rd ch (36 sts).

Fasten off and weave in ends.

STRAWBERRY

Using 3.5mm hook and E, make a magic ring
(see page 117).

Round 1: Ch 1, 5 dc in centre of ring (5 sts).

Round 2: 2 dc in each st (10 sts).

Round 3: (Dc2inc, 1 dc) 5 times (15 sts).

Round 4: Work 1 round straight.

Round 5: (2 dc, dc2inc) 5 times (20 sts).

Round 6: (Dc2tog) 5 times (10 sts).

Round 7: (Dc2tog) 5 times (5 sts).

Using a tapestry needle, weave this yarn
through the last dc sts of the round and
gather together to close the hole. Fasten
off and weave in ends. Using the photograph
as a guide, stitch the leaves of the strawberry
using yarn G and chain stitches (see page 123).

MAKING UP

Sew the top of the cone firmly to the base
of the ice cream. Sew the strawberry firmly
to the centre of the whipped cream and then
sew this securely to the top of the ice cream.

WHIPPY ICE CREAM

Using 3.5mm hook and C, make a magic ring (see page 117).
Round 1: Ch 1, 6 dc in centre of ring (6 sts).
Round 2: 2 dc in each st (12 sts).
Round 3: (Dc2inc, 1 dc) 6 times (18 sts).
Round 4: (2 dc, dc2inc) 6 times (24 sts).
Round 5: 1 dc, dc2inc, (3 dc, dc2inc) 5 times, 2 dc (30 sts).
Round 6: (Dc2inc, 4 dc) 6 times (36 sts).
Round 7: (5 dc, dc2inc) 6 times (42 sts).
Round 8: 3 dc, dc2inc (6 dc, dc2inc) 5 times, 3 dc (48 sts).
Rounds 9–16: Work 8 rounds straight.
Round 17: 3 dc, dc2tog (6 dc, dc2tog) 5 times, 3 dc (42 sts).
Round 18: (5 dc, dc2tog) 6 times (36 sts).
Round 19: (Dc2tog, 4 dc) 6 times (30 sts).
Rounds 20–23: Work 4 rounds straight.
Round 24: 1 dc, dc2tog, (3 dc, dc2tog) 5 times, 2 dc (24 sts).
Rounds 25–27: Work 3 rounds straight.
Stop at this point. Put a safety pin on your working loop.
Using the photograph as a guide, position and secure
safety eyes on the ice cream. Stuff the ice cream firmly.
Then return to finish decreasing, putting the working
loop back on your crochet hook.
Round 28: (2 dc, dc2tog) 6 times (18 sts).
Round 29: Work 1 round straight.
Round 30: (1 dc, dc2tog) 6 times (12 sts).
Round 31: (Dc2tog) 6 times (6 sts).
Using a tapestry needle, weave this yarn through the last
dc sts of the round and gather together to close the hole.
Fasten off and weave in ends. Using the photograph as
a guide, stitch the mouth using black yarn.

CHOCOLATE FLAKE

Using 3.5mm hook and F, ch 8 sts.
Row 1: 1 dc in 2nd ch from hook, 1 dc in each st
to end, turn (7 sts).
Row 2: 1 ch, 1 dc blo in each st to end, turn.
Row 2 forms the pattern. Work a further 9 rows.
Dc the first and last rows together.
Fasten off and leave a long tail. Using a tapestry
needle, weave the yarn through one open side edge.
Stuff the chocolate flake with stuffing. Then sew firmly
to the side of the ice cream.

STRAWBERRY AND RASPBERRY SORBET

Using 3.5mm hook and either H or I, make a magic ring (see page 117).

Round 1: Ch 1, 6 dc in centre of ring (6 sts).

Round 2: 2 dc in each st (12 sts).

Round 3: (Dc2inc, 1 dc) 6 times (18 sts).

Round 4: (2 dc, dc2inc) 6 times (24 sts).

Round 5: 1 dc, dc2inc, (3 dc, dc2inc) 5 times, 2 dc (30 sts).

Round 6: (Dc2inc, 4 dc) 6 times (36 sts).

Rounds 7–10: Work 4 rounds straight.

Round 11: (Dc2tog, 4 dc) 6 times (30 sts).

Round 12: 1 dc, dc2tog, (3 dc, dc2tog) 5 times, 2 dc (24 sts).

Stop at this point. Put a safety pin on your working loop. Using the photograph as a guide, position and secure safety eyes on the ice cream. Stuff the ice cream firmly. Then return to finish decreasing, putting the working loop back on your crochet hook.

Round 13: (2 dc, dc2tog) 6 times (18 sts).

Round 14: (1 dc, dc2tog) 6 times (12 sts).

Round 15: (Dc2tog) 6 times (6 sts).

Using a tapestry needle, weave this yarn through the last dc sts of the round and gather together to close the hole.

Fasten off and weave in ends. Using the photograph as a guide, stitch the mouth using black yarn.

You make me melt

ICE LOLLIES

THERE IS NOTHING MORE WELCOME ON A HOT SUMMER'S DAY THAN A REFRESHING ICE LOLLY. THIS PATTERN IS MADE IN THREE DIFFERENT YUMMY FLAVOURS.

YOU WILL NEED

- Sirdar Happy Cotton, 100% cotton (47yd/43m per 20g ball): yarns A–C listed are for the lolly shown far right.
  1 x 20g ball in 755 Jammy (A)
  1 x 20g 788 Quack (B)
  1 x 20g 786 Yacht (C)
  1 x 20g 773 Sandcastle (D)
- Other lollies use 789 Lippy, 753 Freckle and 780 Treetop or 764 Piggy, 787 Sundae and 777 Cookie for yarns A–C
- 3.5mm (UK9:USE/4) crochet hook
- Polyester stuffing
- Tapestry needle
- A pair of 1/8in (4mm) safety eyes
- Lolly stick
- Strand of black yarn

Tension
Tension is not essential for this project.

Finished Size
Approximately 2in (5cm) wide and 5in (13cm) high.

NOTE The ice lolly is worked in rounds from the top down, using the standard amigurumi technique. The stick is then covered in crochet and the two pieces are sewn together. Place a marker at the beginning of each round so you know where you are in the pattern.

ICE LOLLY

Using 3.5mm hook and A, make a magic ring
(see page 117).

Round 1: Ch 1, 6 dc in centre of ring (6 sts).
Round 2: 2 dc in each st (12 sts).
Round 3: (Dc2inc, 1 dc) 6 times (18 sts).
Round 4: (8 dc, dc2inc) twice (20 sts).
Round 5: (9 dc, dc2inc) twice (22 sts).
Rounds 6–9: Work 4 rounds straight.
Change to B.
Rounds 10–14: Work 5 rounds straight.
Change to C.
Rounds 15–20: Work 6 rounds straight.
Fasten off and leave a 12in (30cm) tail of yarn.
Position the eyes, using the photograph as
a guide. Stitch the mouth using black yarn.

STICK (MAKE 3)

Using 3.5mm hook and D, make a magic ring
(see page 117).

Round 1: 1 ch, 6 dc in centre of ring (6 sts).
Rounds 2–9: Work 8 rounds straight.
Fasten off and weave in ends.

MAKING UP

Push the stick into the cover, then place into
the centre of the lolly. Fill with stuffing. Sew
the base of the lolly together, attaching the
edge to the top of the stick cover as well.

LEMON AND RAINBOW CAKES

THIS WONDERFUL CELEBRATION CAKE HAS MANY LAYERS AND GORGEOUS BUTTERCREAM ICING. MAKE IT SUPER TASTY WITH A DOLLOP OF WHIPPED CREAM AND A SLICE OF LEMON ON TOP. AS A SPECIAL ALTERNATIVE, YOU MIGHT WANT TO MAKE THE RAINBOW VERSION ON PAGE 72.

YOU WILL NEED

- Scheepjes Catona,
  100% mercerized cotton
  (137yd/125m per 50g ball):
  1 x 50g ball in 280 Lemon (A)
  1 x 50g ball in 106 Snow White (B)
  For the Rainbow cake:
- A small amount of 398 Colonial
  Rose (C), 146 Vivid Blue (D),
  205 Kiwi (E), 281 Tangerine (F)
  and 390 Poppy Rose (G)
- 3.5mm (UK9:USE/4) crochet hook
- Polyester stuffing
- Tapestry needle
- Pair of ¹/₈in (4mm) safety eyes
- Strand of black yarn
- Small amount of cardboard

Tension
Tension is not essential for this project.

Finished Size
The cakes are approximately 3in (8cm) wide and 4in (10cm) tall.

NOTE The lemon cake is worked in worked in rounds from the base up, using the standard amigurumi technique. The top of the cake is then made and attached to the sides and puff stitch is used for the piping of the buttercream. Place a marker at the beginning of each round so you know where you are in the pattern.

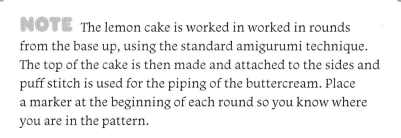

LEMON CAKE

Using 3.5mm hook and A, make a magic ring (see page 117).

Round 1: Ch 1, 6 dc in centre of ring (6 sts).
Round 2: 2 dc in each st (12 sts).
Round 3: (Dc2inc, 1 dc) 6 times (18 sts).
Round 4: (2 dc, dc2inc) 6 times (24 sts).
Round 5: 1 dc, dc2inc, (3 dc, dc2inc) 5 times, 2 dc (30 sts).
Round 6: (Dc2inc, 4 dc) 6 times (36 sts).
Round 7: (5 dc, dc2inc) 6 times (42 sts).
Round 8: 3 dc, dc2inc, (6 dc, dc2inc) 5 times, 3 dc (48 sts).
Round 9: 1 dc in each st blo (42 sts).
Rounds 10–12: Work 3 rounds straight. Change to B.
Rounds 13–14: Work 2 rounds straight. Change to A.
Rounds 15–16: Work 2 rounds straight. Change to B.
Rounds 17–18: Work 2 rounds straight. Change to A.
Rounds 19–22: Work 4 rounds straight. Fasten off and weave in ends.

CAKE TOP

Using 3.5mm hook and B, make a magic ring (see page 117).

Round 1: Ch 1, 6 dc in centre of ring (6 sts).
Round 2: 2 dc in each st (12 sts).
Round 3: (Dc2inc, 1 dc) 6 times (18 sts).
Round 4: (2 dc, dc2inc) 6 times (24 sts).
Round 5: 1 dc, dc2inc, (3 dc, dc2inc) 5 times, 2 dc (30 sts).
Round 6: (Dc2inc, 4 dc) 6 times (36 sts).
Round 7: (5 dc, dc2inc) 6 times (42 sts).
Round 8: 3 dc, dc2inc, (6 dc, dc2inc) 5 times, 3 dc (48 sts).

Do not fasten off. Put a safety pin on your working loop. Using the photograph as a guide, position and secure the plastic eyes and stitch the mouth using black yarn.

Place a small piece of cardboard in the base of the cupcake approx. 2¾in (7cm) in diameter. Firmly stuff the cake.

Joining round: Put the loop back on the hook with the cake side facing sl st the cake top and side together through blo. Fasten off and weave in ends.

PIPED BUTTERCREAM

Using 3.5mm hook and B, attach yarn with a sl st to any stitch of the joining round.

Round 1: (2 ch, 1 puff st in st at base of chain, 1 ch, miss 1 st), (1 puff st in next st, 1 ch, miss 1 st) 23 times (24 puff stitches). Fasten off and leave 12in (30cm) tail of yarn.

WHIPPED CREAM

Using 3.5mm hook and B, make a magic ring (see page 117).

Round 1: Ch 1, 6 dc in centre of ring (6 sts).

Round 2: 2 dc in each st (12 sts).

Round 3: Ch 3 (counts as first st), 2 tr in st at base of ch, 3 tr in each st around, join with a sl st to 3rd ch (36 sts).

Fasten off and weave in ends.

LEMON SLICE

Using 3.5mm hook and A, make a magic ring (see page 117).

Round 1: Ch 1, 8 dc in centre of ring (8 sts).

Round 2: 2 dc in each st (16 sts).

Round 3: (1 dc, dc2inc) 8 times (24 sts). Change to B.

Round 4: 1 dc blo in each st around. Fasten off and weave in all ends. Now fold the circle in half.

Round 5: Join yarn A at right-hand edge of the semi-circle, ch 1 (does not count as a st), 1 dc in each st inserting hook through both layers of fabric to join (12 sts).

Fasten off and weave in ends. Using B, sew two long stitches across rows 1–3 to create segments. Sew securely to the top of the whipped cream.

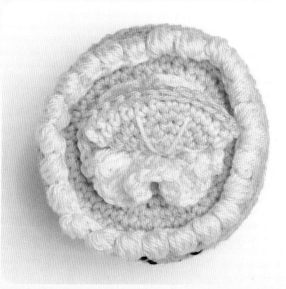

MAKING UP

Fold the puff stitches over towards the centre of the cake and whip stitch the ch stitches to the base of the stitches to form a bobble. Sew the lemon slice firmly to the centre of the whipped cream and then sew this securely to the top of the lemon cake.

CAKE TIME!

RAINBOW CAKE

Using 3.5mm hook and B, make a magic ring
(see page 117).

Round 1: Ch 1, 6 dc in centre of ring (6 sts).

Round 2: 2 dc in each st (12 sts).

Round 3: (Dc2inc, 1 dc) 6 times (18 sts).

Round 4: (2 dc, dc2inc) 6 times (24 sts).

Round 5: 1 dc, dc2inc, (3 dc, dc2inc)
5 times, 2 dc (30 sts).

Round 6: (Dc2inc, 4 dc) 6 times (36 sts).

Round 7: (5 dc, dc2inc) 6 times (42 sts).

Round 8: 3 dc, dc2inc, (6 dc, dc2inc)
5 times, 3 dc (48 sts).

Round 9: 1 dc blo in each st.
Change to C.

Rounds 10–11: Work 2 rounds straight.
Change to D.

Rounds 12–13: Work 2 rounds straight.
Change to E.

Rounds 14–15: Work 2 rounds straight.
Change to A.

Rounds 16–17: Work 2 rounds straight.
Change to F.

Rounds 18–19: Work 2 rounds straight.
Change to G.

Rounds 20–21: Work 2 rounds straight.
Change to B.

Round 22: Work 1 round straight.
Do not fasten off. Put a safety pin on
your working loop.

CAKE TOP

Using 3.5mm hook and C, make a magic ring
(see page 117).

Round 1: Ch 1, 6 dc in centre of ring (6 sts).

Round 2: 2 dc in each st (12 sts).

Round 3: (Dc2inc, 1 dc) 6 times (18 sts).

Round 4: (2 dc, dc2inc) 6 times (24 sts).

Round 5: 1 dc, dc2inc, (3 dc, dc2inc)
5 times, 2 dc (30 sts).

Round 6: (Dc2inc, 4 dc) 6 times (36 sts).

Round 7: (5 dc, dc2inc) 6 times (42 sts).

Round 8: 3 dc, dc2inc, (6 dc, dc2inc)
5 times, 3 dc (48 sts).

Fasten off and weave in ends. Using the
photograph as a guide, position and secure
the plastic eyes and stitch the mouth using
black yarn. Place a small piece of cardboard
in the base of the cupcake approx. 2¾in (7cm)
in diameter. Firmly stuff the cake.

Joining round: Put the loop back on the
hook with the cake side facing, sl st the
cake top and side together through blo.
Fasten off and weave in ends.

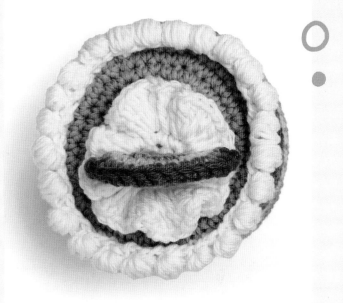

RAINBOW TOPPER

Using 3.5mm hook and C,
make a magic ring.

Round 1: Ch 1, 8 dc in centre of ring. (8 sts).
Change to D.

Round 2: 2 dc in each st (12 sts).
Change to E.

Round 3: (1 dc, dc2inc) 6 times. (18 sts).
Change to A.

Round 4: (2 dc, dc2inc) 6 times. (24 sts).
Change to F.

Round 5: (3 dc, dc2inc) 6 times. (30 sts).
Fasten off and weave in all ends.
Now fold the circle in half.

Round 6: Join yarn G at right-hand
edge of the semi-circle, ch 1 (does not
count as a st) 1 dc in each st working
through both layers of fabric to
join (15 sts).

Make up the cake like the lemon cake
using the piping and the whipped
cream in B.

DOUGHNUTS

THESE RING DOUGHNUTS ARE THE PERFECT CHEEKY TREAT. CHOOSE WHICH ICING AND TOPPING YOU WANT TO ADD. YOU MAY WANT TO GO ALL OUT AND MAKE A CHOCOLATE VERSION WITH GOOEY CHOCOLATE FROSTING.

YOU WILL NEED

- *Stylecraft Naturals Organic Cotton, 100% cotton (114yd/105m per 50g ball):*
  1 x 50g ball in 7187 Flax (A)
  1 x 50g ball in 7188 Wood (B)
  A small amount of:
  7183 Blossom (C)
  7184 Mauve (D)
  7190 Coffee Bean (E)
  7168 Gypsum (F)
  7169 Fondant (G)
  7176 Peach (H)
- *3.5mm (UK9:USE/4) crochet hook*
- *Polyester stuffing*
- *Tapestry needle*
- *Pair of ¹/₈in (4mm) safety eyes for each doughnut*
- *Strand of black yarn*

Tension
Tension is not essential for this project.

Finished Size
The doughnut is approximately 4in (10cm) in diameter.

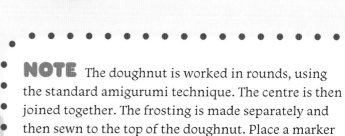

Bite me

NOTE The doughnut is worked in rounds, using the standard amigurumi technique. The centre is then joined together. The frosting is made separately and then sewn to the top of the doughnut. Place a marker at the beginning of each round so you know where you are in the pattern.

DOUGHNUT

Using 3.5mm hook and A, ch 11 and join with a sl st to make a ring.

Round 1: Ch 1, 18 dc in centre of ring (18 sts).

Round 2: Work 1 round straight.

Round 3: (2 dc, dc2inc) 6 times (24 sts).

Round 4: (3 dc, dc2inc) 6 times (30 sts).

Round 5: (Dc2inc, 4 dc) 6 times (36 sts).

Round 6: (5 dc, dc2inc) 6 times (42 sts).

Round 7: 3 dc, dc2inc (6 dc, dc2inc) 5 times, 3 dc (48 sts).

Rounds 8–10: Work 3 rounds straight.

Round 11: 3 dc, dc2tog (6 dc, dc2tog) 5 times, 2 dc (42 sts).

Round 12: (5 dc, dc2tog) 6 times (36 sts).

Round 13: (Dc2tog, 4 dc) 6 times (30 sts).

Round 14: (3 dc, dc2tog) 6 times (24 sts).

Round 15: (2 dc, dc2tog) 6 times (18 sts).

Round 16: Work 1 round straight.

Fasten off and leave a 12in (30cm) tail of yarn. Sew the first and last round together to form a ring. Leave a small hole to stuff the ring. Sew the final stitches of the inner ring together. Weave in ends.

DRIPPING FROSTING

Using 3.5mm hook and C, ch 11 and join with a sl st to make a ring.

Round 1: Ch 1, 18 dc in centre of ring. (18 sts).

Round 2: Work 1 round straight.

Round 3: (2 dc, dc2inc) 6 times (24 sts).

Round 4: (3 dc, dc2inc) 6 times (30 sts).

Round 5: (Dc2inc, 4 dc) 6 times (36 sts).

Round 6: (5 dc, dc2inc) 6 times (42 sts).

Round 7: 3 dc, dc2inc (6 dc, dc2inc) 5 times, 3 dc (48 sts).

Round 8: *3 dc, 3 htr in next st, 3 dc, 4 tr in next st; rep from * 5 more times, 1 sl st in last st.

Fasten off and leave a 12in (30cm) tail of yarn.

PLAIN FROSTING

Using 3.5mm hook and E, ch 11 and join with a sl st to make a ring.

Round 1: Ch 1, 18 dc in centre of ring. (18 sts).

Round 2: Work 1 round straight.

Round 3: (2 dc, dc2inc) 6 times (24 sts).

Round 4: (3 dc, dc2inc) 6 times (30 sts).

Round 5: (Dc2inc, 4 dc) 6 times (36 sts).

Round 6: (5 dc, dc2inc) 6 times (42 sts).

Round 7: 3 dc, dc2inc (6 dc, dc2inc) 5 times, 3 dc (48 sts).

Round 8: Work 1 round straight blo.

Fasten off and leave a 12in (30cm) tail of yarn.

NAUGHTY

MAKING UP

Using strands of yarn F and H, make small straight stitches to replicate hundreds and thousands. Using the photograph as a guide, position the eyes on the surface of the frosting and stitch the mouth using black yarn. Firmly sew the frosting to the top of the doughnut.

Make an additional doughnut using yarn A, and D, with decoration in F and G. Make a plain chocolate doughnut using yarn B and plain frosting using yarn E. With a tapestry needle and a strand of F, chain stitch (see page 123) a line on the top of the frosting. Sew firmly to the top of the chocolate doughnut.

STRAWBERRY CUPCAKE

WE ALL NEED A LITTLE SWEETNESS IN OUR LIFE. A LITTLE STRAWBERRY CUPCAKE WILL BRING JOY TO ANY TEATIME TABLE.

YOU WILL NEED

- *Stylecraft Naturals Organic Cotton, 100% cotton (114yd/105m per 50g ball):*
  1 x 50g ball in 7187 Flax (A)
  1 x 50g ball in 7177 Blush (B)
  A small amount of 7168 Gypsum (C), 7170 Poppy (D) and 7171 Leaf (E)
- *3.5mm (UK9:USE/4) crochet hook*
- *Polyester stuffing*
- *Tapestry needle*
- *Pair of ¹/₈in (4mm) safety eyes*
- *Strand of black yarn*
- *Small amount of cardboard*

Tension
Tension is not essential for this project.

Finished Size
The strawberry cupcake is approximately 2in (8cm) wide and 4in (10cm) tall.

CASE

Using 3.5mm hook and A, make a magic ring (see page 117).

Round 1: Ch 1, 6 dc in centre of ring (6 sts).
Round 2: 2 dc in each st (12 sts).
Round 3: (1 dc, dc2inc) 6 times (18 sts).
Round 4: (2 dc, dc2inc) 6 times (24 sts).
Round 5: (3 dc, dc2inc) 6 times (30 sts).
Round 6: (4 dc, dc2inc) 6 times (36 sts).
Round 7: (5 dc, dc2inc) 6 times (42 sts).
Round 8: Ch 2 (counts as first st), 1 htr blo in each st around, join with sl st to top of ch 2.
Rounds 9–14: Ch 2 (counts as first st), 1 rtrf in each st around.
Fasten off and weave in ends.

CUPCAKE TOP

Using 3.5mm hook and B, make a magic ring (see page 117).

NOTE The cupcake and the case are worked in rounds, using the standard amigurumi technique. The two parts are then joined together to form the full cake. Place a marker at the beginning of each round so you know where you are in the pattern.

Round 1: Ch 1, 6 dc in centre of ring (6 sts).
Round 2: 2 dc in each st (12 sts).
Round 3: (Dc2inc, 1 dc) 6 times (18 sts).
Round 4: (2 dc, dc2inc) 6 times (24 sts).
Round 5: 1 dc, dc2inc, (3 dc, dc2inc) 5 times, 2 dc (30 sts).
Round 6: (Dc2inc, 4 dc) 6 times (36 sts).
Round 7: (5 dc, dc2inc) 6 times (42 sts).
Rounds 8–12: Work 5 rounds straight.
Round 13: 1 dc blo in each st around (42 sts).

Round 14: (5 dc, dc2tog) 6 times (36 sts).
Round 15: (Dc2tog, 4 dc) 6 times (30 sts).
Round 16: 1 sl st, miss 2 sts, 4 tr in next st, miss 1 st, sl st. (miss 1 st, 4 tr in next st, miss 1 st, sl st) rep 8 times (10 shell sts). Fasten off and leave a 12in (30cm) tail of yarn. Using the photograph as a guide, place the plastic eyes and stitch the mouth using black yarn.

FROSTING

Using 3.5mm hook and C, make a magic ring (see page 117).

Round 1: Ch 1, 6 dc in centre of ring (6 sts).
Round 2: 2 dc in each st (12 sts).
Round 3: Ch 2, 1 puff st in same st, 1 ch, (1 puff st in next st, 1 ch) 11 times (12 puff stitches). Fasten off and weave in ends.

STRAWBERRY

Using 3.5mm hook and D, make a magic ring.
Round 1: Ch 1, 5 dc in centre of ring (5 sts).
Round 2: 2 dc in each st (10 sts).
Round 3: (Dc2inc, 1 dc) 5 times (15 sts).
Round 4: Work 1 round straight.
Round 5: (2 dc, dc2inc) 5 times (20 sts).
Round 6: (Dc2tog) 5 times (10 sts).
Round 7: (Dc2tog) 5 times (5 sts).
Using a tapestry needle, weave this yarn through the last dc sts of the round and gather hole together. Fasten off and weave in ends. Using the photograph as a guide, stitch the leaves of the strawberry using yarn E and chain stitches (see page 123).

MAKING UP

Place a small piece of cardboard in the base of the cupcake approx. 2¾in (7cm) in diameter. Sew the bottom of the cupcake firmly to the top of the cupcake case, leaving a small hole to stuff the cake firmly, Finish sewing the two parts together. Sew the strawberry firmly to the centre of the frosting and then sew this securely to the top of the cupcake.

TUCK IN!

SUSHI

THIS SUSHI HAS ALL THE APPEAL OF THE ULTIMATE MODERN SNACK. CHANGE THE COLOURS FOR THE FILLING TO YOUR FAVOURITE FLAVOURS. THE PATTERN HAS FIVE TYPES: THREE RICE NIGIRI WITH DIFFERENT TOPPINGS AND TWO MAKI ROLLS WITH A SEAWEED OUTER.

YOU WILL NEED

- Scheepjes Catona, 100% mercerized cotton (68yd/62m per 25g ball):
  1 x 25g ball in 106 Snow White (A)
  1 x 25g ball in 244 Spruce (B)
  1 x 10g ball in 281 Tangerine (C)
  1 x 10g ball in 518 Marshmallow (D)
  1 x 10g ball in 208 Yellow Gold (E)
  1 x 10g ball in 392 Lime Juice (F)
  1 x 10g ball in 282 Ultra Violet (G)
  1 x 10g ball in 205 Kiwi (H)
- 3.5mm (UK9:USE/4) crochet hook
- Polyester stuffing
- Tapestry needle
- Strand of black yarn

Tension
Tension is not essential for this project.

Finished Size
The nigiri are approximately 2½in (6cm) long, 1in (2.5cm) wide and 6¼in (3cm) tall. The maki rolls are approximately 1½in (3.5cm) in diameter and 1in (2.5cm) tall.

NIGIRI RICE (MAKE 3)

Using 3.5mm hook and A, make 6 ch; work around this central ch to make an oval base to the rice. Work in a continuous spiral, placing a maker in the last st of the round.

Round 1: 1 dc in 2nd ch from hook, 1 dc in each of next 4 ch, 1 ch, 5 dc in other side of each ch, 1 ch (12 sts).

Round 2: 5 dc, (dc3inc) in ch, 5 dc, (dc3inc) (16 sts).

Round 3: 5 dc, (dc2inc) 3 times, 5 dc, (dc2inc) 3 times (22 sts).

NOTE The nigiri sushi with toppers is worked in a oval around a central chain, the topping is made separately and sewn on. The sushi roll is worked in rounds, using the standard amigurumi technique. You start at the centre and then work down the sides and eventually make the base. Place a marker at the beginning of each round so you know where you are in the pattern.

Round 4: Work 1 round straight blo.
Rounds 5–7: Work 3 rounds straight.
Round 8: 5 dc, (dc2tog) 3 times, 5 dc, (dc2tog) 3 times (16 sts).
Round 9: 5 dc, (dc3tog), 5 dc, (dc3tog) (12 sts).
Fasten off and leave a long tail of yarn.
Place some stuffing in the sushi and then using a tapestry needle sew the top of the sushi together; weave in ends.

EGG TOPPING

Using 3.5mm hook and E, ch 7 sts.
Row 1: 1 dc in 2nd ch from hook, 1 dc in each ch to end, turn (6 sts).
Rows 2–12: Work 11 rows straight.
Fasten off and leave a 12in (30cm) tail of yarn.

SEAWEED BAND

Using 3.5mm hook and B, ch 4 sts.
Row 1: 1 dc in 2nd ch from hook, 1 dc in each ch to end, turn (3 sts).
Rows 2–26: Work 25 rows straight (3 sts). Fasten off and leave a 12in (30cm) tail of yarn.

MAKING UP

Using the photograph as a guide, position and embroider some eyes and a moustache on the egg strip using black yarn. Place on top of the rice nigiri and sew in place. Then wrap the seaweed band over both the egg topping and the rice and secure with a few stitches so the band stays in place.

SALMON TOPPING

Using 3.5mm hook and C, ch 2 sts.

Row 1 (RS): 3 dc in 2nd ch from hook, turn (3 sts).

Row 2 (WS): Ch 1, 1 dc, (1 dc, 1 ch, 1 dc) in next st, 1 dc, turn (4 sts).

Row 3 (RS): Ch 1, 2 dc, (1 dc, 1 ch, 1 dc) in next st, 2 dc, turn (6 sts).

Row 4 (WS): Ch 1, 3 dc, (1 dc, 1 ch, 1 dc) in next st, 3 dc, turn (8 sts).

Row 5 (RS): Ch 1, miss st at base of ch, 2 dc, (1 dc, 1 ch, 1 dc) in next st, 2 dc, miss 1 st, 1 dc, turn (8 sts).

Rows 6–11: Rep row 5, 6 times (8 sts). This will create a straight edge. Fasten off and leave a long tail of yarn.

MAKING UP

Using the photograph as a guide, position and embroider some eyes and a mouth on the side of the nigiri rice using black yarn. Take a strand of yarn A and a tapestry needle. With RS facing, backstitch (see page 122) some small stitches between the following rows, 2 & 3, 4 & 5, 6 &7, 8 & 9, 10 & 11. Place on top of the rice nigiri and sew in place.

SHRIMP TOPPING

Using 3.5mm hook and D, ch 7 sts.

Row 1: 1 dc in 2nd ch from hook, 1 dc in each ch to end, turn (6 sts).

Row 2: Work 1 row straight. Change to A.

Rows 3–4: Work 2 rows straight. Change to D.

Rows 5–6: Work 2 rows straight. Change to A.

Rows 7–8: Work 2 rows straight. Change to D.

Row 9: Ch 1, miss st at base of ch, 3 dc, miss 1 st, 1 dc in last st (4 sts).

Row 10: Work 1 row straight. Change to A.

Rows 11–12: Work 2 rows straight. Change to D.

Row 13: Work 1 row straight.

Row 14: Ch 3, 1 tr in st at base of ch, (tr2inc) twice, 1 tr in last st (6 sts). Fasten off and weave in ends.

MAKING UP

Using the photograph as a guide, position and embroider some eyes and a mouth on the side of the rice using black yarn. Place the shrimp on top of the rice nigiri and sew in place.

MAKI ROLL: CARROT AND CUCUMBER

Using 3.5mm hook and C, make a magic ring (see page 117).

Round 1: Ch 1, 5 dc in centre of ring, change to H, 3 dc in centre of ring (8 sts).

Round 2: Change to A, dc2inc in each st around (16 sts).

Round 3: (1 dc, dc2inc) 8 times, (24 sts). Change to B.

Round 4: Work 1 round straight.

Round 5: Work 1 round straight blo.

Rounds 6–10: Work 5 rounds straight. Change to A.

Round 11: Work 1 round straight blo.

Round 12: (1 dc, dc2tog) 8 times (16 sts). Stop at this point. Put a safety pin on your working loop. Stuff firmly. Then return to finish decreasing, putting the working loop back on your crochet hook.

Round 13: (Dc2tog) 8 times (8 sts). Using a tapestry needle, weave this yarn through the last dc sts of the round and gather together to close the hole.

Fasten off and weave in ends.

MAKI ROLL: AVOCADO AND BEETROOT

Using 3.5mm hook and F, make a magic ring (see page 117).

Round 1: Ch 1, 5 dc in centre of ring, change to A, 3 dc in centre of ring (8 sts).

Round 2: Change to G, dc2inc in next st, change to F, (dc2inc) three times, change to A, (dc2inc) four times, each st around (16 sts). Fasten off F and G and continue to work in A.

Round 3: (1 dc, dc2inc) 8 times, (24 sts). Change to B.

Round 4: Work 1 round straight.

Round 5: Work 1 round straight blo.

Rounds 6–10: Work 5 rounds straight. Change to A.

Round 11: Work 1 round straight blo.

Round 12: (1 dc, dc2tog) 8 times (16 sts). Stop at this point. Put a safety pin on your working loop. Stuff firmly. Then return to finish decreasing, putting the working loop back on your crochet hook.

Round 13: (Dc2tog) 8 times (8 sts). Using a tapestry needle, weave this yarn through the last dc sts of the round and gather together to close the hole. Fasten off and weave in ends.

PIZZA AND PIZZA SLICES

PIZZA IS LOVED THE WORLD OVER, SO WHY NOT MAKE YOUR OWN CROCHETED VERSION USING YOUR FAVOURITE TOPPINGS? BRING YOUR PIZZA SLICES TO LIFE BY ADDING A CHEEKY LITTLE FACE.

Take a bite

YOU WILL NEED

- Rico Essentials Cotton DK, 100% cotton (131yd/120m per 50g ball):
  1 x 50g ball in 109 Dust (A)
  1 x 50g ball in 63 Banana (B)
  1 x 50g ball in 02 Red (C)
  A small amount of 66 Grass Green (D),
  90 Black (E), 89 Taupe (F) and 80 White (G)
- Scheepjes Spirit, 44% acrylic, 56% cotton (230yd/210m per 50g ball):
  1 x 50g ball in 311 Butterfly (H)
- 3.5mm (UK9:USE/4) crochet hook
- Polyester stuffing
- Tapestry needle
- Pair of $^1/_8$in (4mm) safety eyes for each pizza slice
- Strand of black yarn

Tension

Tension is not essential for this project.

Finished Size

The pizza is approximately 9$^1/_2$in (24cm) in diameter. Each slice is approximately 4$^1/_2$in (11cm) from the centre to the edge.

NOTE The whole pizza is worked in rounds, using the standard amigurumi technique. The slices are worked in rows. You make the topping separately and attach to the cheese before they are sewn to the pizza base. When working in rounds place a marker at the beginning of each round so you know where you are in the pattern.

PIZZA BASE

Using 3.5mm hook and A, make a magic ring (see page 117).

Round 1: Ch 1, 6 dc in centre of ring (6 sts).

Round 2: 2 dc blo in each st (12 sts).

Round 3: (1 dc, dc2inc) 6 times (18 sts).

Round 4: (2 dc, dc2inc) 6 times (24 sts).

Round 5: (3 dc, dc2inc) 6 times (30 sts).

Round 6: (4 dc, dc2inc) 6 times (36 sts).

Round 7: (5 dc, dc2inc) 6 times (42 sts).

Round 8: (6 dc, dc2inc) 6 times (48 sts).

Continue increasing in this manner for 12 more rounds (120 sts).

Rounds 21–24: Work 4 rounds straight.

Round 25: (18 dc, dc2tog) 6 times (114 sts). Fasten off and leave a 12in (30cm) tail of yarn. Allow the edge of the pizza to roll towards the centre. Sew the last round to round 21 to form a rolled crust. Weave in ends.

CHEESE AND TOMATO TOPPING

Using 3.5mm hook and B, make a magic ring (see page 117).

Round 1: Ch 1, 6 dc in centre of ring (6 sts).

Round 2: 2 dc blo in each st (12 sts).

Round 3: (1 dc, dc2inc) 6 times (18 sts).

Round 4: (2 dc, dc2inc) 6 times (24 sts).

Round 5: (3 dc, dc2inc) 6 times (30 sts).

Round 6: (4 dc, dc2inc) 6 times (36 sts).

Round 7: (5 dc, dc2inc) 6 times (42 sts).

Round 8: (6 dc, dc2inc) 6 times (48 sts).

Continue increasing in this manner for 10 more rounds (108 sts).

Round 19: Work 1 round straight.

Round 20: Ch 2, * 3 tr flo in next st, 2 htr flo in next st; rep from * around sl st in first st. Fasten off and leave a 12in (30cm) tail of yarn.

Round 21: Join yarn C to any back loop of round 19, ch 1, 1 dc at base of ch, 1 dc in each st around. (108 sts).

Round 22: (2 dc, 2 tr in next st) around. Fasten off yarn C and weave in ends.

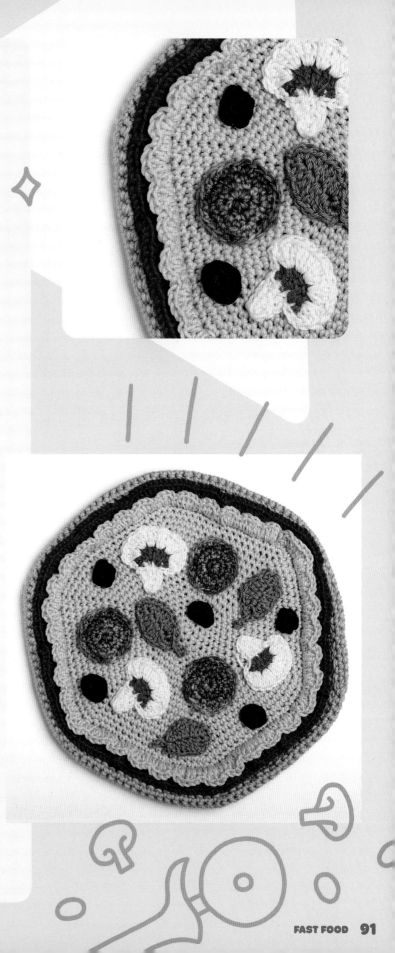

BASIL LEAF (MAKE 3)

Using 3.5mm hook and D, 6 ch, work around this central ch to make an oval base to the leaf.

Round 1: 1 htr in 2nd ch from hook, (1 htr, 1 tr) in next st, 2 tr in next st, (1 tr, 1 htr) in next st, (1 htr, 1 sl st) in next st, 3 ch, 1 sl st in 2nd ch from hook, 1 sl st, (1 sl st, 1 htr) in next st, (1 htr, 1 tr) in next st, 2 tr in next st, (1 tr, 1 htr) in next st, (1 htr, 1 sl st) in last st. Fasten off and leave a 4in (10cm) tail of yarn.

OLIVE (MAKE 5)

Using 3.5mm hook and E, make a magic ring (see page 117).

Round 1: Ch 1, (3 dc, 2 htr, 3 dc, 2 htr) in centre of the ring. Join with a sl st to first ch. Fasten off and leave a 4in (10cm) tail of yarn.

MUSHROOM SLICE (MAKE 3)

Using 3.5mm hook and F, 6 ch.

Round 1: 2 tr in 4th ch from hook, miss 1 ch, 3 tr in next ch, 2 ch, sl st at base of last tr. Fasten off.

Round 2: Join with yarn G to missed ch st in round 1, 5 ch, 1 dc in 2nd ch from hook, 1 dc in each of next 3 ch, 3 ch, 3 tr in the top of turning ch of round 1, 3 tr in each tr of round 1, 3 ch, 1 dc, in each of next 4 ch making the mushroom stalk. Fasten off and leave a 4in (10cm) tail of yarn.

PEPPERONI (MAKE 3)

Using 3.5mm hook and H, make a magic ring (see page 117).

Round 1: Ch 1, 6 dc in centre of ring (6 sts).

Round 2: 2 dc blo in each st (12 sts).

Round 3: (1 dc, dc2inc) 6 times (18 sts).

Round 4: (2 dc, dc2inc) 6 times (24 sts).

Round 5: 1 dc, dc2inc, (3 dc, dc2inc) 5 times, 2 dc (30 sts).

Round 6: (Dc2inc, 4 dc) 6 times (36 sts). Fasten off and leave a 4in (10cm) tail of yarn.

MAKING UP

Using the photograph as a guide, position the pizza toppings on the surface of the cheese and sew firmly using the strands of yarn. Using the tail of yarn from the cheese, sew firmly to the pizza base. You may wish to sew a few small stitches in the centre to ensure that the cheese topping stays securely to the base.

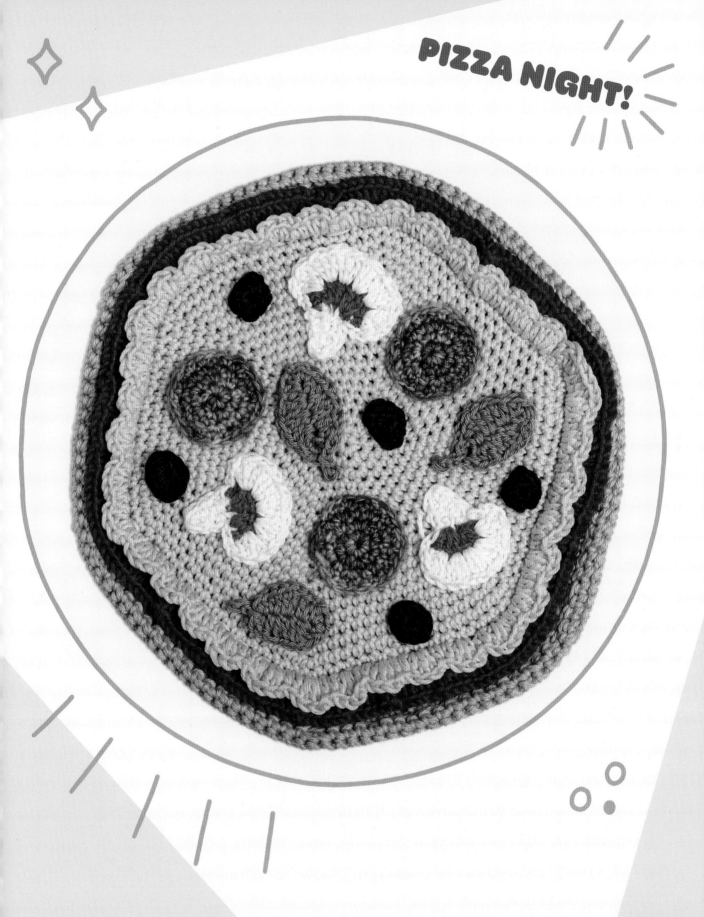

PIZZA SLICE BASE (MAKE 2)

Using 3.5mm hook and A, ch 2 sts.

Row 1: 2 dc in 2nd ch from hook, turn (2 sts).

Row 2: 1 ch, dc2inc in each st, turn (4 sts).

Row 3: 1 ch, 1 dc in each st to end, turn.

Row 4: 1 ch, dc2inc, 2 dc, dc2inc, turn (6 sts).

Row 5: 1 ch, 1 dc in each st to end, turn.

Continue increasing by 2 sts on next and every alternate row until you have 24 sts.

Rows 23–28: Work 6 rows straight, turn (24 sts). Fasten off and leave a long tail of yarn. Roll the last rows over and sew the last row to the base to create a rolled crust.

PIZZA SLICE CHEESE AND TOMATO TOPPING

Using 3.5mm hook and B, ch 2 sts.

Row 1: 2 dc in 2nd ch from hook, turn (2 sts).

Row 2: 1 ch, dc2inc in each st to end, turn (4 sts).

Row 3: 1 ch, 1 dc in each st to end, turn (4 sts).

Row 4: 1 ch, dc2inc, 2 dc, dc2inc, turn (6 sts).

Row 5: 1 ch, 1 dc in each st to end, turn (6 sts).

Continue increasing by 2 sts on next and every alternate row until you have 20 sts.

Fasten off and leave a long tail of yarn.

Row 19: Working all sts flo, 2 ch, 2tr flo in base of ch, 2 htr flo in next st, *3 tr flo in next st, 2 htr flo in next st; rep from * to end. Fasten off and leave a 12in (30cm) tail of yarn.

Row 20: Join yarn C to the back loop of row 18, ch 1, 1 dc at base of ch, 1 dc in each st to end, turn (20 sts).

Round 21: 2 dc, 2 tr in each st to end. Fasten off yarn C and weave in ends.

MAKING UP

Using the photograph as a guide, position and secure the eyes on the surface of the cheese and stitch the mouth using black yarn. Position your choice of pizza toppings on the surface of the cheese and sew firmly using the strands of yarn. Using the tail of yarn from the cheese, sew two sides firmly to the pizza base. Put a small amount of stuffing between the cheese topping and the base. Then sew the final side to the pizza base.

BURGER AND FRIES

THIS MOUTHWATERING BURGER AND BUN COMES COMPLETE WITH LETTUCE AND MELTING CHEESE ON TOP. BUT WHAT WOULD A CHEESEBURGER BE WITHOUT A PORTION OF FRIES?

YOU WILL NEED

- *Scheepjes Catona, 100% mercerized cotton (137yd/125m per 50g ball):*
  1 x 50g ball in 383 Ginger Gold (A)
  1 x 50g ball in 130 Old Lace (B)
  1 x 50g ball in 205 Kiwi (C)
  1 x 50g ball in 208 Yellow Gold (D)
  1 x 50g ball in 390 Poppy Rose (E)
- *Scheepjes Metropolis, 75% wool, 25% nylon (219yd/200m per 50g ball):*
  1 x 50g ball in 066 Copenhagen (F)
- *3.5mm (UK9:USE/4) crochet hook*
- *Polyester stuffing*
- *Tapestry needle*
- *2 x pairs of ⅛in (4mm) safety eyes*
- *2 circles of cardboard, 3¾in (9cm) in diameter*
- *A strand of black yarn*

Tension
Tension is not essential for this project.

Finished Size
The complete burger is approximately 4½in (11.5cm) in diameter and 3in (7.5cm) tall. The carton of fries is approximately 3in (7.5cm) wide and 4in (10cm) tall.

NOTE The burger bun, lettuce and burger are worked in rounds, using the standard amigurumi technique. For the burger, the puff stitches are placed in the spaces between the stitches of the previous round. The cheese slice and the chips are worked in rows. The red carton for the chips is made using a rectangle of crochet worked in rows and then the sides are worked in the round. Place a marker at the beginning of each round so you know where you are in the pattern.

SPECIAL TECHNIQUES

Puff stitch (see page 119): *yo, insert into st, yo and draw loop through st, drawing loop up to the height of 2 ch sts; rep from * twice into the same stitch, 7 loops on the hook, yo and draw loop through all loops on hook. Puff completed.

Puff inc: Work 2 puff sts in one st sp.

Puff2tog: *yo, insert into st, yo and draw loop through st, drawing loop up to the height of 2 ch sts; rep from * twice into the same stitch, 7 loops on the hook, rep into next st sp, yo and draw loop through all 14 loops on hook. Puff dec completed.

YUM!

BUN TOP

Using 3.5mm hook and A, make
a magic ring (see page 117).

Round 1: 1 ch, 7 dc into the centre of the ring.

Round 2: 2 dc into each st (14 sts).

Round 3: (dc2inc, 1dc) 7 times (21 sts).

Round 4: (2 dc, dc2inc) 7 times (28 sts).

Round 5: 1 dc, dc2inc, (3 dc, dc2inc) 6 times,
2 dc (35 sts).

Round 6: (dc2inc, 4dc) 7 times (42 sts).

Round 7: (5 dc, dc2inc) 7 times (49 sts).

Round 8: 3 dc, dc2inc (6 dc, dc2inc) 6 times,
3 dc (56 sts).

Round 9: (dc2inc, 7dc) 7 times (63 sts).

Round 10: (8 dc, dc2inc) 7 times (70 sts).

Round 11: (34 dc, dc2inc) twice (72 sts).

Rounds 12–15: Work 4 rounds straight.
Stop at this point. Put a safety pin
on your working loop.

BUN BASE

Using 3.5mm hook and A, make a magic ring
(see page 117).

Round 1: 1 ch, 8 dc into the centre of the ring.

Round 2: 2 dc into each st (16 sts).

Round 3: (dc2inc, 1dc) 8 times (24 sts).

Round 4: (2 dc, dc2inc) 8 times (32 sts).

Round 5: 1 dc, dc2inc, (3 dc, dc2inc)
7 times, 2 dc (40 sts).

Round 6: (dc2inc, 4dc) 8 times (48 sts).

Round 7: (5 dc, dc2inc) 8 times (56 sts).

Round 8: 3 dc, dc2inc (6 dc, dc2inc)
7 times, 3 dc (64 sts).

Round 9: (dc2inc, 7dc) 8 times (72 sts).

Round 10: Work 1 round straight.

Rounds 11–12: Work 2 rounds straight tbl.
Fasten off and weave in ends.

BUN INSIDES
(MAKE 2)

Using 3.5mm hook and B, make a magic ring
(see page 117).

Round 1: 1 ch, 8 dc into the centre of the ring.

Round 2: 2 dc into each st (16 sts).

Round 3: (dc2inc, 1dc) 8 times (24 sts).

Round 4: (2 dc, dc2inc) 8 times (32 sts).

Round 5: 1 dc, dc2inc, (3 dc, dc2inc)
7 times, 2 dc (40 sts).

Round 6: (dc2inc, 4dc) 8 times (48 sts).

Round 7: (5 dc, dc2inc) 8 times (56 sts).

Round 8: 3 dc, dc2inc (6 dc, dc2inc)
7 times, 3 dc (64 sts).

Round 9: (dc2inc, 7dc) 8 times (72 sts).

Round 10: Work 1 round straight.
Fasten off and weave in ends.

MAKING UP

Using the photograph as a guide, position
and secure safety eyes on the top of the
bun. Stitch the mouth using black yarn.
Taking a length of yarn B, stitch some large chain
stitches on the top of the burger bun to represent
seeds. Stuff the top of the bun firmly. Cut a circle
of cardboard, approximately 3½in (9cm) in
diameter. Place the cardboard on top of the
stuffing. Then place one bun inside on top.
Putting the working loop of yarn A back on
your crochet hook, dc the last row of the top
half and the last row of the bottom half together.
Fasten off and weave in ends. For the base, place
two pieces of card inside the burger bun base.
Place one bun inside on top and using yarn B
and with the inside facing, dc the last rounds
of the inside and the burger base together.
Fasten off and weave in ends.

LETTUCE

Using 3.5mm hook and C, make
a magic ring (see page 117).

Round 1: 1 ch, 8 dc into the centre of the ring.

Round 2: 2 dc into each st (16 sts).

Round 3: (dc2inc, 1dc) 8 times (24 sts).

Round 4: (2 dc, dc2inc) 8 times (32 sts).

Round 5: 1 dc, dc2inc, (3 dc, dc2inc) 7 times,
2 dc (40 sts).

Round 6: (dc2inc, 4dc) 8 times (48 sts).

Round 7: (5 dc, dc2inc) 8 times (56 sts).

Round 8: 3 dc, dc2inc (6 dc, dc2inc) 7 times,
3 dc (64 sts).

Round 9: 2 ch (this counts as 1 st), 2 tr at base
of ch, work 3tr in each st around. Join with
a sl st to the top of ch sts.

Fasten off and weave in ends.

BURGER

Using 3.5mm hook and F, make
a magic ring (see page 117).

Round 1: 1 ch, 8 dc into the centre of the ring.

Round 2: 1 puff in each st (8 puffs).

Round 3: (2 puff inc next sp) 8 times (16 puffs).

Round 4: 1 puff in each sp (16 puffs).

Round 5: (1 puff, 2 puff inc in next sp)
8 times (24 puffs).

Round 6: 1 puff in each sp (24 puffs).

Round 7: (2 puff, 2 puff inc in next sp)
8 times (32 puffs).

Round 8: 1 puff in each sp (32 puffs).

Round 9: (2 puff, puff2tog) 8 times (24 sts).

Round 10: 1 puff in each sp (24 puffs).

Round 11: (1 puff, puff2tog) 8 times (16 sts).

Round 12: 1 puff in each sp (16 puffs).

Round 13: (puff2tog) 8 times (8 sts).

Using a tapestry needle, weave this yarn
through the last sts of the round and gather
hole together. Fasten off and weave in ends.

SLICE OF CHEESE

Using 3.5mm hook and D, ch 21 sts.

Row 1: 2 dc in 2nd ch from hook,
1 dc in each st to end, turn. (20 sts).

Rows 2–22: Work 21 rows straight,
turn (24 sts).

Fasten off and weave in ends.

MAKING UP

You can leave your burger so all the
parts can be separated. Or secure
together working a long stitch through
the centre of the burger bun top, cheese,
burger, lettuce and then burger bun base.

ENJOY!

FRIES (MAKE 8)

Using 3.5mm hook and D, ch 21 sts.

Round 1: 1 sl st in 2nd ch from hook, 1 sl st in each st to end, turn. (20 sts).

Rounds 2–4: 1 sl st in each st to end, turn.
Fasten off and weave in ends.

CARTON FOR FRIES

Using 3.5mm hook and E, ch 6 sts.

Round 1: 1 dc in 2nd ch from hook, 1 dc in each ch to end, turn (5 sts).

Rounds 2–14: Work 13 rows straight.
Do not fasten off; you will now work around the edges of the crochet in continuous rounds.

Round 1: Ch 1, 5 dc, work 14 dc down the row ends of the crochet, 5 dc along the foundation ch, and 14 dc along row ends of the second edge (38 sts).

Rounds 2–7: Work 6 rounds straight.

Round 8: (Dc2inc, 12 dc, dc2inc, 5 dc) twice (42 sts).

Rounds 9–14: Work 6 rounds straight.
Fasten off and weave in ends.

CARTON INSIDE

Using 3.5mm hook and E, ch 8 sts.

Round 1: 1 dc in 2nd ch from hook, 1 dc in each ch to end, turn (7 sts).

Rounds 2–16: Work 15 rows straight.
Fasten off and leave a 12in (30cm) tail of yarn.

MAKING UP

Using the photograph as a guide, position and secure safety eyes on the front of the carton. Stitch the mouth using black yarn. Stuff the carton firmly. Then place the carton inside on top of the stuffing. Sew this piece of crochet about two rounds below the edge of the carton, using small whip stitches (see page 124). Fold each chip in half and secure to the carton inside with some small stitches.

CRISPY

FRIED EGG

AN EGG MAKES THE MOST BRILLIANT BREAKFAST AND LOOK HOW CHEEKY IT LOOKS ON THE PLATE. PUT IT IN YOUR BURGER FOR AN EXTRA TREAT.

Time for brunch!

YOU WILL NEED

- Scheepjes Catona, 100% mercerized cotton, (68yd/62m per 25g ball):
  1 x 25g ball in 208 Yellow Gold (A)
  1 x 25g ball in 106 Snow White (B)
- 3.5mm (UK9:USE/4) crochet hook
- Polyester stuffing
- Tapestry needle
- Pair of $^1/_8$in (4mm) safety eyes
- Strand of black yarn

Tension
Tension is not essential for this project.

Finished Size
The egg is approximately $3^1/_2$in (9cm) wide and $4^1/_4$in (11cm) long.

NOTE The egg is worked in rounds, using the standard amigurumi technique. Place a marker at the beginning of each round so you know where you are in the pattern.

FRIED EGG FRONT

Using 3.5mm hook and A, make a magic ring (see page 117).

Round 1: Ch 1, 6 dc in centre of ring (6 sts).
Round 2: 2 dc in each st (12 sts).
Round 3: (Dc2inc, 1 dc) 6 times (18 sts).
Round 4: (2 dc, dc2inc) 6 times (24 sts).
Round 5: 1 dc, dc2inc, (3 dc, dc2inc) 5 times, 2 dc (30 sts).
Rounds 6–7: Work 2 rounds straight. Change to B.
Round 8: (Dc2inc, 4 dc) 6 times (36 sts).
Round 9: (5 dc, dc2inc) 6 times (42 sts).
Round 10: 3 dc, dc2inc (6 dc, dc2inc) 5 times, 3 dc (48 sts).
Round 11: (7 dc, dc2inc) 3 times, 1 htr, 2 tr, 1 dtr, 2 tr, 1 htr, dc2inc, (7 dc, dc2inc) twice (54 sts).
Round 12: 4 dc, dc2inc, (8 dc, dc2inc) twice, 2 htr, 3 tr, 1 dtr, dtr3inc, 1 dtr, 3 tr, 2 htr, dc2inc, (8 dc, dc2inc), 6 dc (61 sts).

Fasten off and weave in ends. Place safety eyes using the photograph as a guide or stitch the eyes and mouth using black yarn.

FRIED EGG BACK

Using 3.5mm hook and B, make a magic ring
(see page 117).

Round 1: Ch 1, 6 dc in centre of ring (6 sts).

Round 2: 2 dc in each st (12 sts).

Round 3: (Dc2inc, 1 dc) 6 times (18 sts).

Round 4: (2 dc, dc2inc) 6 times (24 sts).

Round 5: 1 dc, dc2inc, (3 dc, dc2inc) 5 times,
2 dc (30 sts).

Fasten off and leave a 12in (30cm) tail of yarn.

MAKING UP

Put a small amount of stuffing in the back of
the yolk, place the back over the stuffing and
then use the tail of yarn to whip stitch (see page
123) the last row of the back to row 8 of the yolk.

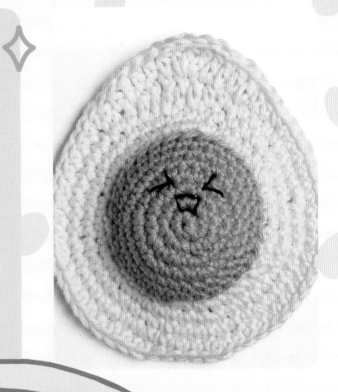

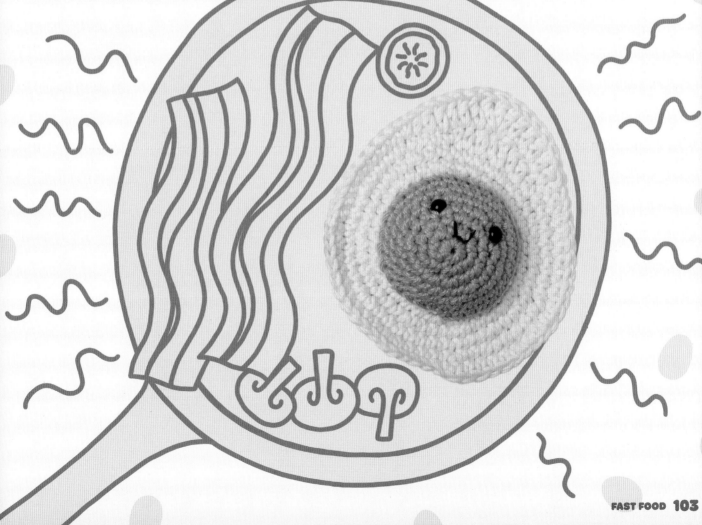

HOT DOG

THIS YUMMY HOT DOG HAS ITS OWN CROCHETED BUN.
WHAT TOPPING WILL YOU PUT ON, KETCHUP OR MUSTARD?

YOU WILL NEED

- Scheepjes Catona, 100% mercerized cotton (137yd/125m per 50g ball):
  1 x 50g ball in 383 Ginger Gold (A)
  1 x 50g ball in 406 Soft Beige (B)
  1 x 50g ball in 388 Rust (C)
  A small amount of 208 Yellow Gold (D) and 390 Poppy Rose (E)
- 3.5mm (UK9:USE/4) crochet hook
- Polyester stuffing
- Tapestry needle
- Pair of 1/8in (4mm) safety eyes
- Thin cardboard
- Strand of black yarn

Tension

Tension is not essential for this project.

Finished Size

The completed hot dog is approximately 6in (15cm) long.

NOTE The hot dog bun inside and outside are worked in an oval, working around a central foundation chain using the standard amigurumi technique. Place a marker at the beginning of each round so you know where you are in the pattern.

HOT DOG BUN OUTER (MAKE 2)

Using 3.5mm hook and A, make 25 ch; work around this central ch to make an oval base to the bun. Work in a continuous spiral, placing a maker in the last st of the round.

Round 1: 1 dc in 2nd ch from hook, 1 dc in each of next 23 ch, 1 ch, 24 dc in other side of each ch, 1 ch (50 sts).

Round 2: Dc2inc, 22 dc, (dc2inc) 3 times, 22 dc, (dc2inc) twice (56 sts).

Round 3: Dc2inc, 23 dc, (dc2inc, 1 dc) 3 times, 22 dc, (dc2inc, 1 dc) twice (62 sts).

Rounds 4–7: Work 4 rounds straight.
Fasten off and weave in ends.

HOT DOG BUN INNER (MAKE 2)

Using 3.5mm hook and B, make 25 ch, work around this central ch to make an oval base. Work in a continuous spiral, placing a maker in the last st of the round.

Round 1: 1 dc in 2nd ch from hook, 1 dc in each of next 23 ch, 1 ch, 24 dc in other side of each ch, 1 ch (50 sts).

Round 2: Dc2inc, 22 dc, (dc2inc) 3 times, 22 dc, (dc2inc) twice (56 sts).

Round 3: Dc2inc, 23 dc, (dc2inc, 1 dc) 3 times, 22 dc, (dc2inc, 1 dc) twice (62 sts).

Fasten off and weave in ends.

HOT DOG SAUSAGE

Using 3.5mm hook and C, make a magic ring (see page 117).

Round 1: Ch 1, 6 dc in centre of ring (6 sts).

Round 2: 2 dc in each st (12 sts).

Round 3: (Dc2inc, 1 dc) 6 times (18 sts).

Rounds 4–32: Work 29 rounds straight.

Stop at this point. Put a safety pin on your working loop. Stuff firmly. Then return to finish decreasing, putting the working loop back on your crochet hook.

Round 33: (1 dc, dc2tog) 6 times (12 sts).

Round 34: (Dc2tog) 6 times (6 sts).

Using a tapestry needle, weave this yarn through the last dc sts of the round and gather together to close the hole. Fasten off and weave in ends.

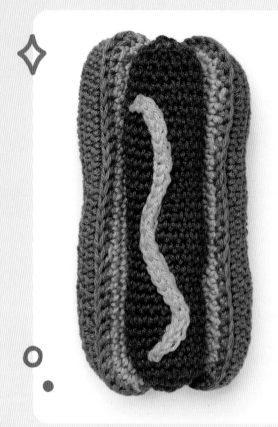

KETCHUP OR MUSTARD
(MAKE 8)

Using 3.5mm hook and either D or E, ch 32 sts.
Row 1: 1 sl st in 2nd ch from hook, 1 sl st in each st to end, turn (31 sts).
Fasten off and weave in ends.

MAKING UP

Using the photograph as a guide, position and secure safety eyes on the outer of the hot dog bun. Stitch the mouth using black yarn. Place a bun inner on some thin cardboard, draw round the outside of the shape. Cut out two cardboard inners.

Stuff the bun outer. Place the cardboard on top of the stuffing. Then place the bun inner on top. With the outer of the bun facing and using yarn A, dc the last row of the top half and the last row of the outer and inner bun together. Fasten off and weave in ends. Repeat for the second bun half. Along one side of the hot dog bun, sew the two halves of the bun together. Place the hot dog inside. Position the mustard or ketchup along the side of the hot dog and, using small stitches, sew in place.

You can leave your hot dog and bun so all the parts can be separated. Or secure together, working stitches along the side of the bun and sausage so they are kept in place.

GETTING STARTED

ALL THE TOOLS AND MATERIALS YOU WILL NEED TO USE TO CREATE YOUR CUTE CROCHETED FOOD ARE EXPLAINED HERE, ALONG WITH ESSENTIAL KNOW-HOW ON ABBREVIATIONS AND CONVERSIONS.

CROCHET HOOKS

Crochet hooks come in a range of materials and sizes. In this book, I use a wide range of sizes according to the thickness of the yarn. For size 3.5mm or 3mm I like to use an ergonomic metal-pointed crochet hook.

YARN

I love to work in a range of yarns: from the most expensive merino for soft baby blankets through to hard wearing cottons for toys and homeware. The key issue with making cute items is to find a yarn which has a vibrant colour or replicates the tones of the food. For items that will be played with, cotton is always a good option as it can easily be cleaned.

You certainly don't have to go out and buy large balls of yarn. These days, yarn producers are making very small amounts, which are perfect for small projects like these at a dainty 20g or 25g.

ACRYLIC AND FASHION YARNS

For some of the items I have small balls of polyester chenille yarn. This has a very fluffy texture and is great for making super cute toys. It is not as easy to see where the stitches are, so I use my fingers to find the next gap where the hook should go.

STUFFING

I have used Minicraft Supersoft toy stuffing to stuff the food. This material complies with BS145, BN5852 and EN71 standards and is safe for children. Make sure the food is stuffed so that it is firm but not bulging, as this will distort the look of the overall piece.

PLASTIC SAFETY EYES

For most of the food in this book, I have used ⅛in (4mm) plastic safety eyes. They come in two parts: the eye with a shank to push through the crochet and then a plastic washer which fits very securely over the shank inside the item. Once the washer has been added it is very hard to dismantle. My advice is to make sure you have placed your eyes where you want them, perhaps even fill the item with a little stuffing to ensure they are in the right position, before you attach the washer. Once you have pushed both parts of the eyes together, give them a tug test. Try to pull them out so you can make sure they are fixed securely.

NEEDLES

You will need a variety of needles for completing the projects, including a tapestry needle for sewing in ends and adding details.

WIRE

Using wire in items that will be played with by children is not a good idea. But on a number of items I have used some very thin floristry wire for stalks. Only use this if the item is ornamental and just for display. In every case make sure your wire is not poking out of your food so it does not hurt you or any inquisitive admirer of your work.

TIP You can use any yarn you like for these projects. In general I have used a DK weight with a 3.5mm hook. But you could create a mini version using a sock yarn or lace-weight yarn and 2.5mm hook or go gigantic and create a huge cupcake footstool with a super chunky and 9–15mm hook. I warn you, though – chunky yarns are quite physically demanding to work with. You will feel as if you have done a full workout!

ABBREVIATIONS

alt	alternate
blo	back loop only
ch	chain
ch sp	chain space
cm	centimetres
cont	continue
dc	double crochet
dc2inc	double crochet increase by one stitch
dc2tog	double crochet two stitches together (decrease by one stitch)
dc3tog	double crochet three stitches together (decrease by two stitches)
dec	decrease
DK	double knitting
dtr	double treble
dtr2inc	work 2 dtr into same st
flo	front loop only
g	grams
htr	half treble
htr2inc	work 2 htr into same st
in	inch(es)
inc	increase
m	metre(s)
mm	millimetre(s)
pm	place marker
rep	repeat
RS	right side
rtrf	raised treble front
sl st	slip stitch
sp	space
st(s)	stitch(es)
tbl	through the back loop
tog	together
tr	treble
tr2inc	work 2 tr into same st
tr2tog	treble crochet two stitches together (decrease by one stitch)
yd	yard(s)
yo	yarn over
yrh	yarn round hook
WS	wrong side

UK AND US DIFFERENCES

Some UK and US terms have different meanings, which can cause confusion, so always check which style the pattern you are using is written in. This will ensure that your crochet develops correctly. There is nothing more frustrating than working on a pattern, then realizing it is all wrong and needs to be unravelled. This book is written in UK crochet terms.

UK crochet terms	US crochet terms
Double crochet	Single crochet
Half treble	Half double crochet
Treble	Double crochet
Double treble	Triple crochet
Treble treble	Double triple crochet

CONVERSIONS

Crochet hook sizes

UK	Metric	US
14	2mm	B/1
13	2.25mm	B/1
12	2.5mm	C/2
–	2.75mm	C/2
11	3mm	D/3
10	3.25mm	D/3
9	3.5mm	E/4
–	3.75mm	F/5
8	4mm	G/6
7	4.5mm	7
6	5mm	H/8
5	5.5mm	I/9
4	6mm	J/10
3	6.5mm	K/10.5
2	7mm	K/10.5
0	8mm	L/11
00	9mm	M–N/13
000	10mm	N–P/15

CROCHET TECHNIQUES

IN THIS SECTION YOU CAN LEARN THE BASIC TECHNIQUES NEEDED FOR THE PROJECTS IN THIS BOOK. SOME WILL NEED A BIT OF PRACTICE, BUT ONCE YOU HAVE LEARNT THEM YOU CAN MAKE AN ARRAY OF CROCHET EDIBLES.

HOLDING A HOOK

Hold your hook in either your right or your left hand as you would a pen, in between your index finger and thumb.

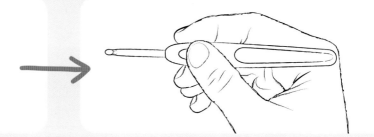

HOLDING YARN

With the hand you are not using to hold the hook, wrap the yarn around your little finger and then drape the yarn over your hand. You can hold the tail of your yarn between the middle finger and your thumb and use your index finger to control the yarn.

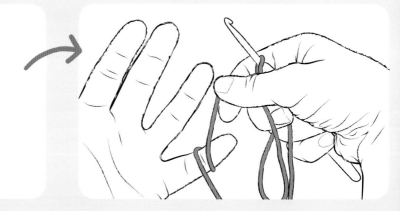

MAKING A SLIP KNOT

Make a loop of yarn over two fingers. Pull a second loop through this first loop, pull it up and slip it onto your crochet hook. Pull the knot gently so that it forms a loose knot on the hook.

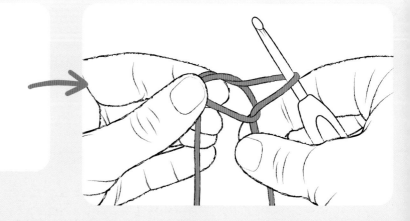

CHAIN STITCH (CH ST)

1. Start with a slip knot on the hook.

2. Wrap the yarn over the hook.

3. Pull the loop through the loop of the slip knot to form one chain stitch.

SLIP STITCH (SL ST)

This stitch is ideal for decoration and for attaching two pieces of crochet together.

1. Insert the hook into a stitch and wrap the yarn over the hook.

2. Draw the loop through the stitch and the loop on the hook. Continue in this way for the required number of slip stitches.

1.

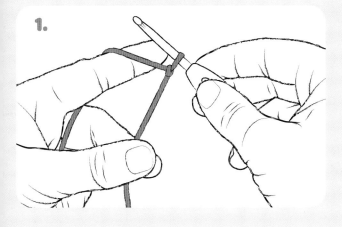

2.

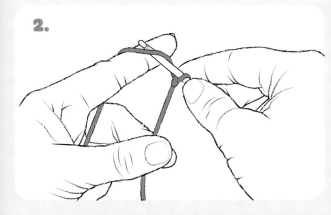

3.

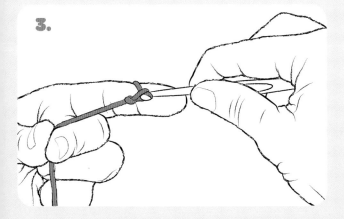

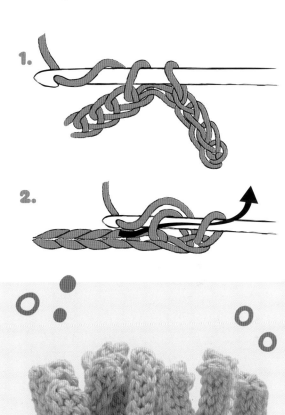

DOUBLE CROCHET (DC)

1. Insert the hook through the stitch, yarn over the hook, and pull through the stitch. There will be two loops on the hook.

2. Wrap the yarn over the hook and pull through both loops on the hook. There will be one loop left on the hook.

HALF TREBLE (HTR)

1. Wrap the yarn over the hook, insert the hook through the stitch, yarn over the hook and pull through the stitch. There will be three loops on the hook.

2. Wrap the yarn over the hook again and draw through all the loops on the hook. There will be one loop on the hook.

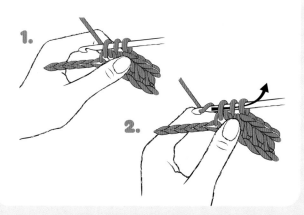

TREBLE CROCHET (TR)

1. Wrap the yarn over the hook and insert the hook through the stitch. Wrap the yarn over the hook and pull through the stitch.

2. Wrap the yarn over the hook and pull through two loops. There will be two loops on the hook.

3. Wrap the yarn over the hook again and pull through the remaining two loops. There will be one loop left on the hook.

DOUBLE TREBLE (DTR)

1. Wrap the yarn over the hook twice, insert the hook through the stitch, yarn over the hook and pull through the stitch. There will be four loops on the hook.

2. Wrap the yarn over the hook and pull through two loops. There will be three loops on the hook.

3. Wrap the yarn over the hook and pull through two loops. There will be two loops on the hook.

4. Wrap the yarn over and pull through the remaining two loops. There will be one loop on the hook.

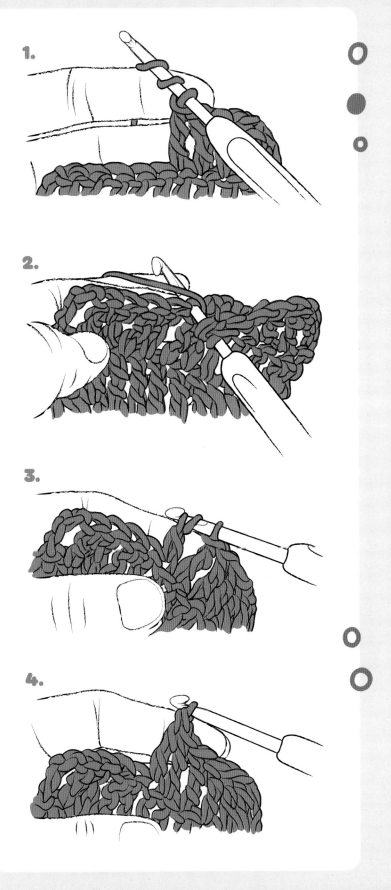

1.

2.

3.

4.

You can do it!

WORKING IN ROWS

When making straight rows, you need to make a turning chain at the beginning of the row for the stitch you are working on. A double crochet row will need one chain at the beginning of the row; this will be indicated in the pattern.

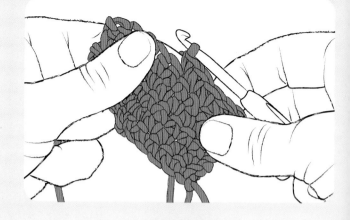

WORKING IN ROUNDS

One wonderful thing about crochet is that you don't always have to work in rows; you can also work in rounds. The majority of the patterns in this book are worked in continuous spiral rounds with no slip-stitch joins or turning chains.

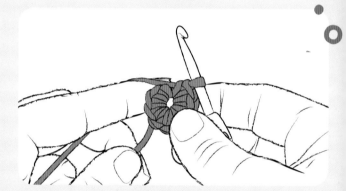

WORKING IN SPIRALS

Most of the patterns in this book are worked in spiral rounds, beginning with a magic ring. They are worked using the amigurumi crochet technique, crocheting in a continuous spiral with no slip-stitch joins or turning chains. In this you can create one seamless cyclindrical shape.

In order to know where each row starts it is advisable to place a marker at the beginning of each row.

MAGIC RING

This is a neat way of starting a circular piece of crochet while avoiding the unsightly hole that can be left in the centre when you join a ring the normal way. Magic rings are nearly always made with double crochet stitches, as this creates a tight, dense crochet fabric.

1. Start by making a basic slip knot. Pull up the loop and slip this loop onto your crochet hook.

2. Before you tighten the ring, wrap the yarn over the hook (outside the circle) and pull through to make the first chain.

3. Insert the hook into the ring, wrap the yarn over the hook and pull through the ring so there are two loops on the hook.

4. Wrap the yarn over the hook again (outside the circle) and pull through both loops.

5. You have made your first double crochet stitch.

6. Continue to work like this for as many double crochet stitches as are stated in the pattern instructions. Pull the yarn tail to tighten the ring and then continue working in the round as usual.

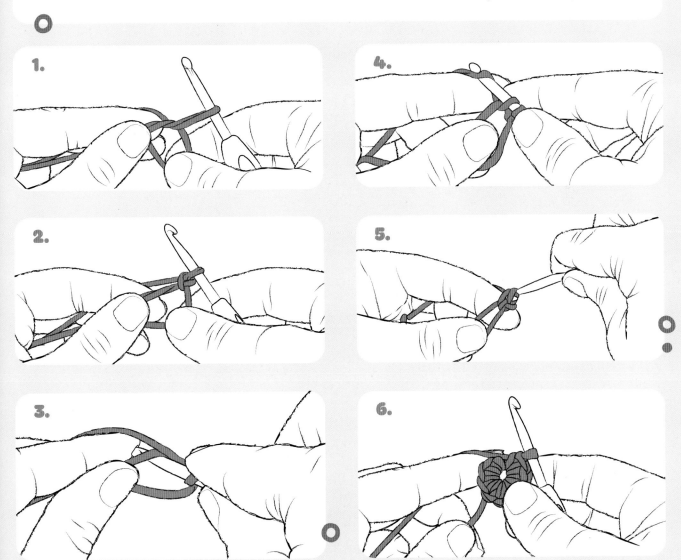

INCREASING (INC)

Work a stitch as normal, then work another into the same stitch of the previous row.

DECREASING (DC2TOG)

1. Insert your hook into the next stitch, pull a loop through, insert your hook into the next stitch, and pull a loop through.

2. Wrap the yarn over the hook and pull the yarn through all three loops.

1.

2.

PUFF STITCH

The burger pattern (see page 97) creates a puff by drawing several loops together and then making a sl st in the first ch of the stitch.

1. Yarn over your hook, insert you hook into the next st.

2. Yarn over and draw the loop through, draw it up to the height of 2 ch sts.

3. Rep twice into the same stitch. You will have 7 loops on your hook. Yarn over and draw through all loops on the hook. Make 1 chain st to secure.

WORKING INTO THE BACK LOOP (BLO)

Generally, a crochet stitch is made by slipping the hook under the top two loops of a stitch. However, you can also create a different effect by working into the back loop only of each stitch of one round or row. This creates a ridge or horizontal bar across the row. In this book I have used this technique for several projects in this book, including the Pumpkin (page 48).

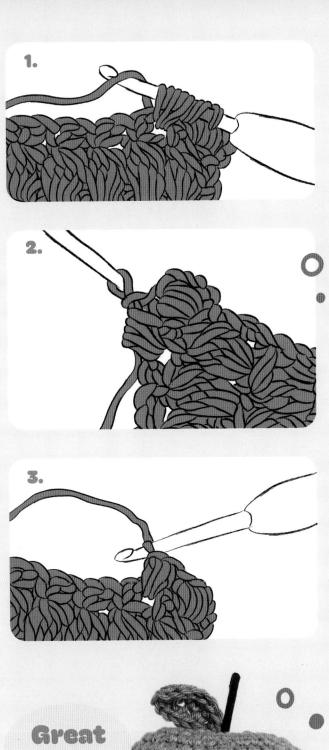

1.

2.

3.

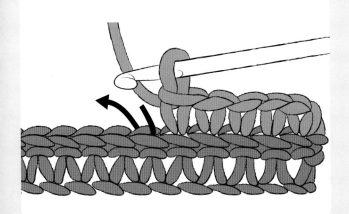

Great job!

CRAB STITCH

Crab stitch gives a neat finish, creating the effect of a corded edge. I have used this technique for the top of the ice-cream cones (see page 59). It is made by working double crochet in the opposite direction from normal, that is, from left to right. It can feel slightly awkward to work but is worth persevering with.

1. With RS facing, insert the hook from front to back into the stitch immediately to the right of the last one. Point the hook slightly downwards and catch the yarn at the back. Bring the yarn through the stitch. Wrap the yarn round the hook and draw it through the two loops.

2. Repeat to the end of the row.

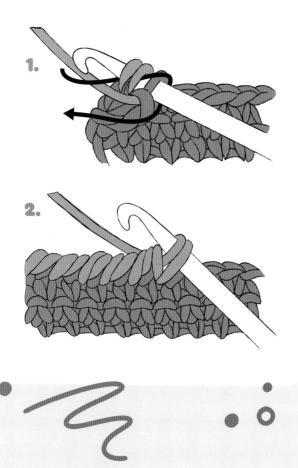

RAISED TREBLE FRONT (RTRF)

This is a brilliant technique for creating texture and does give a ribbed effect which I have used for the cupcake cases (see page 78). You work your crochet hook around the stitches created on the previous row.

1. Wrap the yarn over the hook and insert your hook from front to back around the post of the next stitch.

2. Wrap the yarn over the hook and pull the yarn through so that you have three loops on your hook. Wrap the yarn over the hook and pull through all three loops.

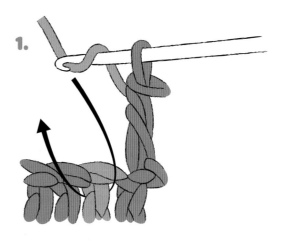

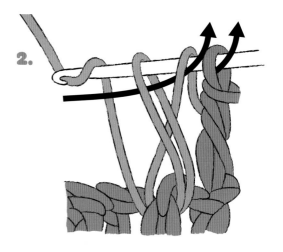

FINISHING TOUCHES

THIS SECTION SHOWS YOU HOW TO MAKE UP YOUR FINISHED PROJECT SO THAT IT IS ROBUST AND DURABLE. I HAVE USED EMBROIDERY TECHNIQUES FOR EXTRA DETAIL. YOU WILL NEED A TAPESTRY NEEDLE AND SOME YARN TO SEW THESE STITCHES ONTO THE SURFACE OF YOUR PIECE.

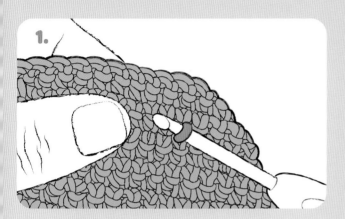

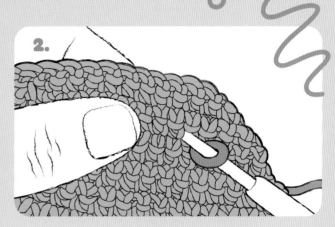

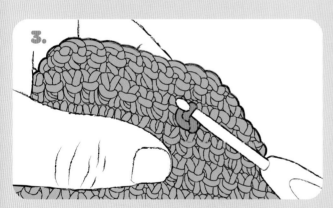

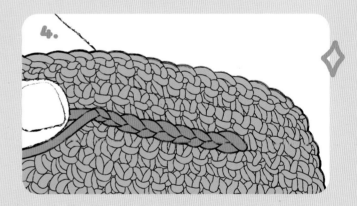

SLIP-STITCH SURFACE DECORATION

You can create a neat line where two colours meet by working a slip stitch between the two rows.

1. Hold the yarn on the wrong side the of the fabric and draw a loop up between the stitches.

2. Then push your hook down into the next stitch to hook another loop.

3. Bring this loop up through your first loop to create a chain stitch effect using crochet.

4. To fasten off, cut the yarn and pull through to the front through the last loop. Then using a tapestry needle take the yarn back down the the wrong side over the loop, weave in this end to secure.

CREATING CHARACTER ON THE FACES

You can create different features, by taking co-ordinating yarn and place a small stitch under the eyes and then take the needle the back of the head. Once you pull the yarn, the face will change shape. Experiment to see how the nose will become emphasised. Use thin embroidery thread to sew small stitches for eyelashes.

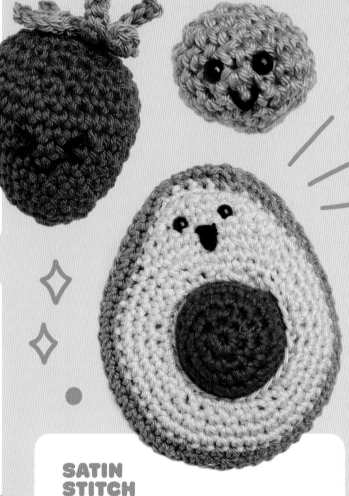

BACKSTITCH

Backstitch is excellent for creating a straight line and creating the expression of the mouth. Using the illustration as a guide, bring your needle up through the fabric at A and then push the needle back down at B, bring the needle up again at C, and then down again at A. Work backwards like this to create a neat continuous line.

SATIN STITCH

Satin stitch is used to fill in a larger area of embroidery. I have used satin stitch for the mouth of the avocado (see page 38). Make long stitches right next to each other.

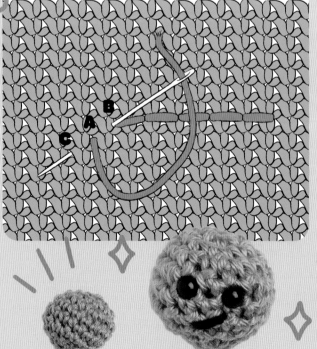

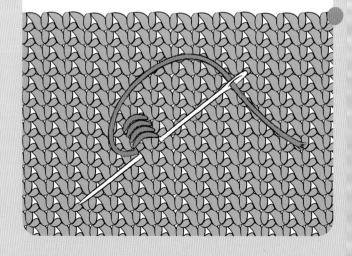

FRENCH KNOT

French knots are ideal for sewing eyes or dots onto your food. Bring your needle up through the fabric and then wrap your thread around the needle three times. Then insert the needle back into the fabric very close to where it emerged.

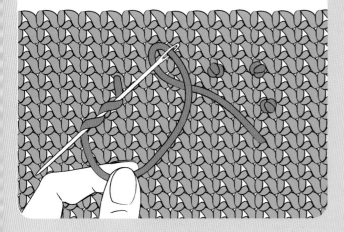

CHAIN STITCH

Bring your needle up through the fabric and hold the thread down with your thumb. Insert the needle back into the fabric where the needle emerged and then bring the tip back out a short distance along, making sure the thread caught by your thumb is under the needle. Pull the thread through to create a loop. Repeat this process to create more chains, by inserting the needle again close to where it emerged. For the final chain, hold in place with a tiny stitch over the end of the loop.

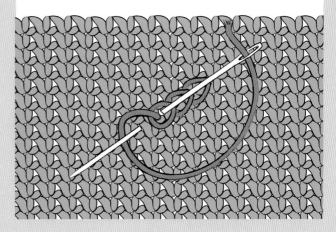

SLIP-STITCH SEAM

Place the pieces of the crochet together with wrong sides facing each other. Insert the hook through both pieces at the beginning of the seam and pull up a loop, then chain one stitch. Work a row of slip stitches by inserting your hook through both sides at the same time.

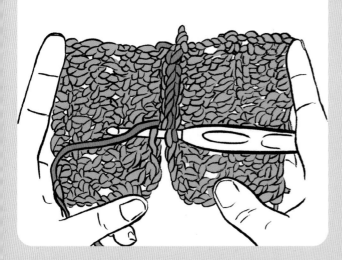

DOUBLE CROCHET SEAMS

Work as for a slip-stitch seam but working double crochet instead of slip stitch.

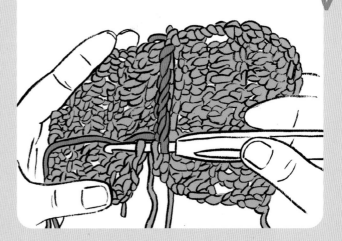

WEAVING IN ENDS

Try to leave about 8in (20cm) of yarn when you fasten off. You may be able to hide the tail in your next row. I always ensure that my ends have been woven backwards and forwards three times.

1. Thread the remaining yarn end onto a blunt tapestry needle and weave in the yarn on the wrong side of the project. Work along the stitches one way, then work back in the opposite direction.

2. Weave the needle behind the first ridge of crochet for at least 2in (5cm). Snip off the end of the yarn close to the fabric of the crochet.

WHIP STITCH

You can use whip stitch to sew two layers of fabric together. Make a knot at the end of your yarn. Bring your needle from the wrong side through to the right side of your fabric, then hold both pieces of your fabric together, wrong sides facing each other. Push your needle from the back piece through to the front piece, and repeat evenly along the edge. There will be a row of small stitches along the edge of your work, joining both pieces together.

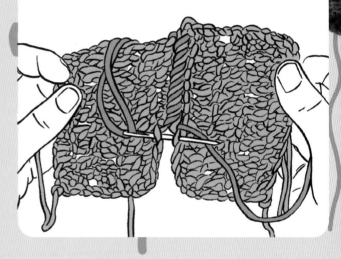

1.

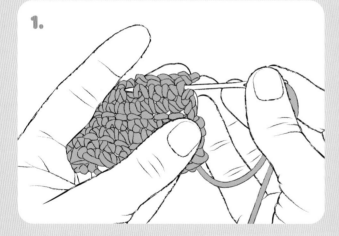

2.

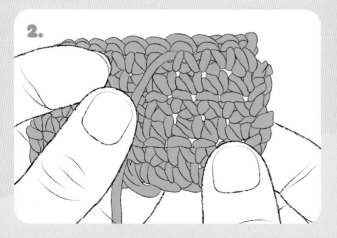

Hooray!

For my godson Oliver (Spud)

ACKNOWLEDGEMENTS

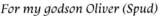

The moment I made the very first cupcake for this book I was hooked. My mind started whirring... what else could I make? Much of the enjoyment of creating these patterns has been shared with the wonderful team at GMC. They have a passion and dedication to ensure their craft books are the very best and I am fortunate to work with them. Thank you to my editor Virginia and also to Jonathan Bailey, the publisher who trusts me to come up with appealing projects. Thanks must also go to the wonderful illustrator and designer Emily Hurlock and Andrew Perris for the photography. Thank you also to Rachel Vowles, who did a wonderful job checking the patterns.

I would like to thank a number of yarn producers and retailers for their support: thanks to Stylecraft Ltd and the team at Spa Mill, Annabelle and Juliet, who generously donate many of the yarns. Thanks to Sara and the team at Black Sheep Wools for their ongoing support and for being a fab yarn shop.

I continue to love and enjoy the support and encouragement of my crafty best friends Lucy (Attic 24) and Christine (Winwick Mum) – they believe I have a yarn time machine to make all this crazy stuff in.

I am grateful that my family who join me in laughing and getting excited by the mad things I create. Benjamin, Robert and of course Stanley, I love you.

First published 2023 by
Guild of Master Craftsman Publications Ltd
Castle Place, 166 High Street, Lewes,
East Sussex BN7 1XU
United Kingdom

ISBN 978-1-78494-660-9

A catalogue record for this book is available from the British Library.

Publisher **Jonathan Bailey**
Production Director **Jim Bulley**
Design Manager **Robin Shields**
Senior Project Editor **Virginia Brehaut**
Designers **Emily Hurlock, Rhiann Bull**
Illustrator **Emily Hurlock**
Pattern checker **Rachel Vowles**
All photography by **Andrew Perris**, except on pages 108–109
from Shutterstock.com

Colour origination by GMC Reprographics
Printed and bound in China

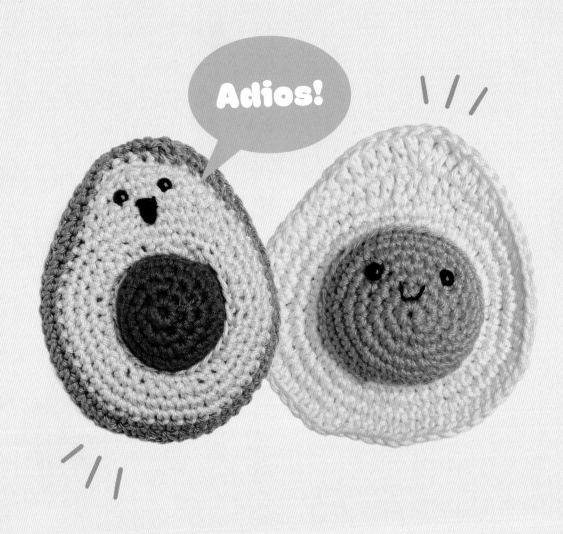

GMC Publications Ltd
Castle Place, 166 High Street,
Lewes, East Sussex
BN7 1XU
United Kingdom
Tel: +44 (0)1273 488005
www.gmcbooks.com